A LEARNED CITY

By the same Author

*

THE SAVAGE DAYS

SCHOOL IN PRIVATE

THE BARRICADES

TEA WITH MRS GOODMAN

THE GARDEN TO THE SEA

FRIENDS APART

PANTALOON

TWO BROTHERS

A Learned City

The Sixth Day of the
Valediction of Pantaloon

by

Philip Toynbee

1966

CHATTO & WINDUS

LONDON

Published by
Chatto & Windus Ltd
40 William IV Street
London W.C.2

*

Clarke, Irwin & Co Ltd
Toronto

Printed in Great Britain
by T. A. Constable Limited
Hopetoun Street Edinburgh

A Learned City

Old
Abberville

Ho artifice and passion!
Passionate memory held by artifice
And grafted to the young green stalk of Olaf.
I spoke in verses yesterday,
In poems planted like the round mosaic of a pavement,
Each a devised assault on the mind of attentive Olaf.
Oh my amanuensis, sick-bed attendant, legatee,
How I contrive for you:
How I distil in the stained retorts of an old mind
Eau de Vie; firewater; rainbow drops that hold
A distant lifetime and a lost history!
"In boastful vein tonight, the Ancient Mariner."
I caught the pursed lips of affronted modesty
And heard the valley's soft indulgent groan.
But don't be alarmed, my boy.
You won't hear much today of these debased archaic tones;
For I mean to let others speak for me—
Or rather to speak through the mouths of two who are long dead—
Professor Nielson in the year of his retirement and
That young idiot of an undergraduate.
I mean his grandson:
I mean the young man who used to caper under my name.
Do you remember—but of course you do—
How I spoke to you once—was it the third or the second day?—
Of an old city—yes, "the city of my birth and learning"?
Wait!
"Friends supine on the lawn," I said, or something like it,
"And enemies cursing from the stairs.
"A city of elegant obscenity,
"Of foaming malice and sweet nights of solitary labour:
"Dryer than deserts;
"Damp as the smell of mud and thyme
"And the rincing of the bells on fluent mornings."
A premature and partial vision:

5

A felicitous abbreviation;
A trailer, only, for the long film
That I meant you to see and ponder later on.
Now you shall see it whole, Oxford in the fourth decade,
Ancient Oxford as the years have brightened and diminished it.
All the radiance of the city and all the fumes of its fires
Have been emprismed by my years and artifice,
Gathered into my burning-glass
To fall upon your golden topknot here and now.
  Famous Professor Nielson broods in his college room
  In the month of his most unwilling retirement.
  A raging old Lear of spire and quad,
  As you shall hear,
  Who even regrets, in the days of his black and yearning misan-
  thrope,
  Boar and wolf, "the banished beasts of the hill",
  And that rough prehistoric age
  When never a don had yet breathed the valley air.
  (You've never known
  Implacable Tory yearners such as he.)
As for the grandson, that chameleon
And parrot of his betters' tunes,
I've set him walking through the streets and meadows of old Oxford,
Out of his own college first of all
And back at last to the college of his Patroclus
After three years and all the four seasons.
And I guess that communication between the two
Will be at best devious;
Often numbed and muffled;
At worst warped by all the waves of time and the air.
(We know something, eh my green corn-stalk of the West,
My captive audience, my unwilling heir,
Of how such waves may surge between
An old yearning man and a youth who swims in present time.)
  But hear him now, Professor Kurt Nielson,
  And then my monstrous, many-coloured avatar.

* * *

6

A LEARNED CITY

A dying dog, damn it: a rented house, and unbequeathed:
A house unguarded—hear the window shudder! Who shall
have it?
Professor Emeritus! He shakes to death in a cold corner:
Professor Emeritus! Water drops have stained my cheeks.
But watch, you grubs of the black gown, how Njal dies:
Watch how Nielson goes to the dark, eh you *worming* dons.

   A dying dog, he bristled still at the nightly ghost of the boar:
All night he whined for the printless spoor of the wild wolf.
Out of his cold muzzle foams a cloudy blossom of blood:
His eye is cold with rheum: his sparky hide is dull and
dusty.
But how he scuttered the snow when the trees were rimed
with red frost:
He scattered the leaves, seeking a buried spoor of dead
beasts.
I mourn for the banished beasts of the hill; kings of ancient
snows:
And I do mourn this western hound who sniffs for a lost age.
But eh, to devil and hell, I say, with the bores of the port
decanter!
Soused in old Oporto; fumed and fogged in blue Havana.

    Fuming Grampa!
      A tiptoe, entering the quad,
      The grandparental quad, I
      Lift a bunched gown to my face.
      Fie, fie to hide my phiz,
      My gross mug as I teeter past
      The viking eye, the brass halloo
      Of Nielson at his window!
      But instead of the ex-prof I see
      Only the stained chapel wall.
    Hail silence! Cunning be my guide!

Gunnar's dog had died to warn him, split in half by Thorkel:

So shall my dog die, to tell of his master's near death.
A tenant-dog—unhappy beast!—he wailed at the far hoofs:
He heard from afar the Bailiff-Bursar clopping atop the hill.
Don and devil! Hear what he sang as he spurred his spumy
horse:
"*I'll* unhorse, at last, that arrogant old totem of our brother-
hood."
　　"Pray you, sir," he crooned, "dismount and yawn your days
　　away:
　　"Be easy, sir, to yearn away in a *well-merited* idleness."
　　(Aye, he'd potter me to death, the wormy envoy of my
　　college.)
　　"Twiddle your mind and broken pen, milord, to a sleepy
　　death."

　　　　Shame on the impious, muffled head
　　　　Turned so unkindly away
　　　　From the yawning gaffer aloft on the third stair!
　　　　　　But how he makes me yearn, love,
　　　　　　For Spain, or even far Cathay:
　　　　　　Seville's arborescent glow
　　　　　　And a mandarin munching
　　　　　　A mandarin.
　　　　Down, sir, down! The poor devil,
　　　　To whom I owe my roaring brain,
　　　　Is exiled; is exiled!
　　　　Oh lament for Nielson banished
　　　　To his mild suburban hill!

Forty years I yearned for a yeoman's holding, a safe strong-
hold:
Aye, to *hold* at last my own demesne of stone and tree.
And sons would yearly sprout on the hill as trees creak to the
sky:
New sons, dragon's teeth, grow from the yeasty soil.
　　I saw him once, the Boer farmer, leaning upon his gate:

A LEARNED CITY

A matted bison, all beard against his burning farm.
Alive, his heart swelled with the sap of the corn and the
buried root:
And when he died his huge thigh-bone hummed on his own
hill.

My heart a pitter-pat . . . but *there*!
The gate attained, and grieving Grampa
Cruelly, ah cruelly thwarted.
    And now the mist is dripping-white
    In the eyeless, dark canal.
    Black walls sweating in
    The drowning air of Oxenford.
    And there a burning bolshevic,
    Plotting, sulks along the wall.
    "Hail Varley, full of woe!"

For Nielson never fared by choice down the far seas:
Fared no further overland than the burning city of Novgorod.
And yet my sons—Hendrik! Nils!—shall have no heritage:
Lucky sons were they to die before I left them nothing.
And now I'm reft of all but that gold-plated son:
A nothing he, but gilded tin and a puff of stale perfume.

Christian! He was a golden lad.
Still his glorious match recalled
With rapturous fingers flicked in the air.
And I'm his undisputed heir
On the battlefield of Twickenham.
Nothing can stale it, Nuncle Chris,
The muddy tingling as the light
Dies between the roaring stands.
    But ah Matthew Miles, my sweet conscience,
    Beautiful and virtuous,
    How you wince and hold your ears

9

Whenever Abberville begins
To blow on his own base trump.
Pitiful, vainglorious Abberville!
(But the right man, though I *do* say,
The best possible fellow to lead the pack.)

And now they mock me: now they'd geld me. Smelly monkey-
men!
Raw behinds and fusty fur that's sharp with stink of lice.
This banderlog has mimed the grief of graven governors:
"Out of our hands, alas—and ah, 'tis grievous so to lose you!
"But from our deep distress, sir, grant you the house you hovel
in now, sir:
"Until your doom, sir, live at the golden favour of the college."
Such as *you*, a shamble through the windy autumn quad:
Becreaséd palms have brushed the dew. Eh, 'tis a windy ape!

Billy Barnes, I mean to *say*,
Shambler of the windy fields,
Honest, lofty-hearted kerl—
Honestly now, grant me this—
Don't I possess—be frank with me!
A certain *brio* which you lack?

And down in the Woodstock Road the crabby-yellow women
pray:
Hear them pray my knell, hunched to swoop on Boar's Hill.
Vinegar-vultures! Grey wattles droop in a steam of tea:
Creased like the grey birds that hung in the wind of the High
Veld.
A gabled house; blue tiles; mullioned; misbegotten:
The house of a dead or fled brood where only the dam cackles.
But even upon this house of death they cast their yellow eyes:
Lidless eyes have shot a sulphured light from the Woodstock
Road.

Miss Bannion; Mrs Brook; Miss Wade. Watching all night:
Miss Wade; Miss Bannion; Mrs Brook. Hark for Nielson's
rattle!
I've seen the black-widow Brook shake her dusty feathers:
Beaks clash at garden walls: fouled feathers fly.
  But I shall *live* until the unnatural hags burst inward:
  They shall cave in, squeezed by the air of angry rooms.
  And though my occupation's gone I shall grin to see it:
  Grin again to see it. And I shall do such things ... I'll do ...

    Drip-drop, dribble-drop
    From a yellow Bridge of Sighs
    Where the glassy students clatter.
      Grampa, occupation gone,
      Must fret his empty days away
      On Boar's Hill, on Boar's Hill.
      (But how he bores me, *bores* me with his grievances!)

I am a most dream-harrowed wretch. Oh the fools!
Fools forget the yellow boy who slumbers in my head.
Buried boy of Folda, leave the snoring South behind!
Far beyond Folda crush the resinous woods of Finmark.

    Boys are beasts, and that's a fact,
    And Abberville's a beastly boy,
    A boiling beast of a boy.
    (Squeeze out his glistening Etnas.)
    By what *folie de grandeur*,
    What pipsqueak impertinence,
    Do you abuse your grandfather,
    And then—his brash epigone—
    Snore in his company?
      And Billy Barnes is better than I am; noble and kindly,
      Rightly loved by all who ever followed his leadership,
      Calm in defeat, in victory never absurdly elated.

Whereas R. Abberville lumbers from the doldrums to
the seventh heaven;
Glooms in defeat and hulks from the field like a petu-
lant schoolboy;
In victory chants too loud in the steamy vaults of the
baths.

Ancient fancies! Dreaming fancies! I have sucked from dreams:
Oh I could melt and mould you all again—easily, easily!
Standing aloft in our tower I make Magdalen a mammoth:
I fashion distant Worcester into a green-blazing galleon.
A pirate on his own poop, lo, I take captive all colleges:
I board Balliol with one blink of devil-blazing eyes.
  But best I see the oldest town of tiles and square towers:
  The little learned dorp of steep roofs and rough walls.
  Shepherds lean on their crooks, in Meadows, beyond old
  Merton:
  Kine sway in the grassy High to the clatter of iron bells.
And yet in Merton's stone they delight only in the Decorated:
They swoon at the Baroque glories of a jacobean Baptist.
Rococo entrances them, and even the false gothic "amuses"
them:
They delight in *any* debasement of what was once sturdy and
strong.
They shudder with a cold shock as they skurry across Mob
Quad:
Oh *brutal* the bare barn! *Horrid* the fell fall of the roof!
And how they'd all moan at Michael's harsh stone tower
If ever they *saw* th'embattled Saxon in the din of motors.
Who but I daily renews his sap from the rough stones;
Renews at a soiled noon the speckless light of the first morning?
Whatever softens from an early strength, this they swoon upon:
Melted or mingled things; whatever twists from a straight line.
  So do they melt and twist the gravéd columns of the law
  As a doric column was twirled into a stick of sugar-candy.
  Good and ill are mixed and moulded to a grinning gargoyle:
  Adultery! Simples mixed in a pot of green filth.

"Christian!" A whisper in the mist.
But whether my uncle's meant, or that
Pilgrim of the early day,
Both, *both* are better than I.
Shining gold or tarnished, Uncle Chris
Is a better man than his bloody nephew is.
No such twisted, envious apprentice,
No such swollen frog as I;
But an old unhappy bull
Deflated by the banderillas
Of his own self-scrutiny.
  Oh *bloody* Abberville!

The night was not yet fouled when the wolf wailed on Shot-over:
'Twas clear night when the hog's eyes were burning Wytham woods.
Until from creaky branches broke this hueless hulk of apes:
Hueless hulkers of the swollen brow and fatted brain.
  Now HODGETT stands for hog; for Whitefang, cackling WADE.
  Hodgett of candy and cabal; Wade with snuff and snot beslobbered.
  A devil's don, stuck by a sweet tooth in crunched toffee:
  Another whose very sweetness rots like sweets in a foul tooth.
  Hodgett a lean lemon above the walnut and the candle-flames:
  Wade a red walrus: both reek of the rotted grape.
  Claws uncreak to clutch the slobbered butts of grey leaf:
  Hodgett's fat fingers clutch the purple dregs of Douro.
Ah that the beasts were howling yet on windy Cumnor's bent:
May they hunt and howl again, and feast on these fellows.
The wolf shall be crunching shoulder-of-Wade and lean haunch-of-Hodgett:
Dons shall be devilled by wolf-scullions; soused in the smokey grape.

Twilight fell on the sweet prince
Who once astride an emperor sat.
(Hark to the carillon, pray,
For perfumed Alcibiades!)
A pocked stone head—*that* one, surely—!
Fretted by the mists of Isis,
Bore my charming uncle
Long, long ago.
    Prince of the Feast when Pleasure was king
    Christian dined at the Chatham Club—
    Corinthian were the candle-sticks.
    Or, on a windy April morning,
    Rode the head of a black emperor—
    A Caesar riding his Augustus—
    And argent Oxford bags were flapping
    In the breezes of the Broad.

I saw my own son lurk with ABEL down the Turl:
I saw them skulk, greasing votes, from B.N.C. to Corpus.
From Brazen Nose to Body of Christ where worm and weevil
toil:
BANNION's devils crackle: Abel scurries across the High.

    Fellow and faun, capricious don,
    Crackling under Capricorn;
    Book-worm in the northern light
    But faring to the south in winter.
        I have desired to live my student days
        In the sunny Garden Quad,
        Beside the crafty filigree
        Of Abel's garden gate.
    (Do you dance by moonlight in the spring,
    Apollinax the Younger?
    Upon the mound of jonquils in the spring,
    Mister Apollinax?)

I saw how the plague spread—plot, whisper, counter-plot:

A LEARNED CITY

I saw Abel pour his poison into ROUGHTON's rough ear.
This inky squid of learning quivers in every slithy limb:
A quiver of lies throbs through all the veins of the university.
See that vine which twists like a green snake from college to
college?
See how the sap of plot and cuckle creeps along the tendrils?
A place of learning? A vast boudoir all abuzz with spite:
A board where bishops bend their cloven heads to nodding
knights.
I see a court where every cardboard jack grins in a closet:
Jack to knave, they swap betrayals of rank, suit and number.
Oh, fallen are all the spires! The dream dies! The bells are
dumb!
Books are banged shut, and the old boar of the hill is dying.

> Elegant dialectician,
> Deft confuter of fogies,
> How your pointed ears quiver
> In the buzz of High Table,
> Thou *subdolous* Jack Abel!
>> But Abel, if the truth were known,
>> Is neither Bannion's man nor Wood's
>> In the coming war of succession
>> To ex-Professor Nielson's chair.
>> For Bannion, though a man of true learning,
>> Precise and scholarly,
>> Is barbarously puritanical.
>> And Wood, the favoured candidate
>> Of Grampa for his own succession,
>> Shares, it seems, his mentor's predilection
>> For the ornate embellishment of texts.
> A pant of warm and bookish air
> And Blackwell's door has thudded on
> A spotted lady, blinking in the mist.
> PERKIN WARBECK—gold on green—
> A Study of his Life and Times.
> Hail King Perkin,

Werbecque, royal lord
Of Flanders mud!

But BERNARD, you I sing from all the crumbling towers of
Oxford:
Bernard Carew, my true son: eh, my honest ancient.
Carew! Carew! The wounded witness! Sweet Carew, my son!
One-legged, with grained face, friend of the dead sons.
  He heaves his sea-log down the Broad like an old salt of the
  Main:
Scholar of Ypres, he was sent down from fiery Festubert.
And can you sweeten my gall, Bernard, galled by war and
wife?
But a man steeled by the storm of steel. Shall we sit silent
together?
He gave Bannion a bit of his burning mind. Ho, I heard it!
Der Bannion yelped and fled; fled yelping from Wadham to
Worcester.

  Well the hubby is indeed
  A boiteur, sans doute,
  Give the devil his due,
  And ohne Zweifel a Frontkämpfer.
  The grained-with-powder face,
  The trenched and mined face
  Recalls the turmoil of the air
  At Festubert.
    But when she sighs, "Bernard! Ah! Alas!"
    I frankly
    RETCH.
    My grampa's best man and most loyal
    Skirmisher in
    This game of the Musical Chair.
  "Morning, Vernon! Morning, Tom!"
  Two Christian epicenes
  Trip like skittish nuns across
  A road shrill with bicycles.

Bannion! A mere microscope! A master of the crammed
margin!
What does Bannion see but foxed page and faded ink-stain?
Fevered eyes are gummed to parchment: Bannion's dry quill
Collates, collates, collates, collates till sea and heaven heave.
    And all the scribes whose veins run vitriol and caustic-soda:
    The humble scribes who seethe in the sour vats of their
    humbleness.
All who gribble and graft in the ash of fires their fathers lit:
The new school of the Young Dead—*all* praise Bannion.
BLISS likewise. What did Bernard call the fat fellow?
"Silenus in a flock of fallen cherubs." Filthy fellows!

      "Well, the hubby is indeed
      "A boiteur, sans doute!"
        You make me *sick*, you make me so
        Sick of your posing and your ghastly
        Don Juanish, Casanovish,
        Ladies'-mannish, womanising . . .
      Liquescent Bliss, Nielson's foe,
      Swirls from the gate of Trinity
      With fallen jowls averted from
      The blast of foggy air that blows
      Out of the trumpet of the Turl.
        "My policy, sir, will be justice tempered with pre-
        judice."
        A doggy don whose croaks and quips,
        Minted at Sunday noon
        By Bliss, Maître de Salon,
        Become by the Sabbath following
        The universal currency of wits.

PROUT, the Easter lamb, of milky mien and bland belief:
How can I trust the churchy voice and hands like cold lamb?
Prout could learn more of his fallen god from the night wind
Than ever he learned by scratching like an old hen in Jerome's
dust.

On the other hand we know that graecian JOLIFFE is a true
man:
Shrivelled pippin; russet man; hesiodic farmer.
Chaste of mind; scrubbed stone and unpolished pine:
He bears a faint scent of balsam, clean, sweet and herbal.
And if to Joliffe I should whisper . . . say that Prout would
vote . . .
    That's sure—Prout would vote as Joliffe told him to. . . .
Stink of snakes! Shall *Nielson* plot in dirty corners?
Laocoon in dirty coils! Nay, I'll *pike* the python!
Hell is peopled by professors; ruled by wardens, deans and
masters:
Dons with gowns ablaze cackle at blazing whelps and sizors.
Vice-chancellor Satan maddens the students with a bad text:
"Knowledge serves itself alone, and naught beyond itself."
And famished are they by such a feed of dry, dusty bonemeal:
Parched by the dust they wet their whistles at the stew of
gossip.
For those who feed on variorum sicken of print and paper:
They sick it up, and suck at every lip for honied scandal.
    And which of our Crown Jewels is still ungrained by the
    black dust?
    Which of our royal scholars seeks today for gold in ashes?
    Regius Professor FORD, world-master of mathematics,
    Are *you* seeking still for the golden balance of the world?
    FARQUAR, ancient historian, cackling hen of the new coop:
    He layed, at last, a new text of someone's old edition.

        Today's task—the elimination of metaphysics,
   —   A gathered library of old-gold nonsense,
        The stored honey of many a bee-loud bonnet.
            According to Abel Grampa's free version of the sagas
            Excruciates meticulous scholars by
            Its shameless liberties and gross empurplement.

Measure the scholars by their bellies, wolf-shanks and goitres:
Good grief, the sunken shanks of *that* dwarfish philosopher!

What mean, mizzling thoughts must seethe in Abel's horny
hump!
What parched and scrannel "propositions" squeak from his
wind-pipe!

> Wolf, we long ago agreed
> Never to think a dwarf must keep
> A dwarfish soul; or that a giant
> Is of heaven's company
> Because his head has touched the sky.

Fifty shrunk to nineteen; thirty-one defaulting:
Thirty-one were bored with "the Prof", and came no more to
hear him.
And of this rump eight, if you please, were puffed and spotted
females:
Aye, *they* stick, knowing my love for learned ladies!
> But once I packed the lecture-halls with more than Murray
> could:
> Four hundred faces flowered in Merton hall below me.

> And Wolf, without . . .

But all Oxford, now, is a carcase of bright yellow maggots,
Or a sour, mouldered loaf where *red* maggots bore and breed.
The tang of spite and envy, sweetened with good-fellowship.
"Comrades!" Dwarfs who dull the bells and stink the streams
of Oxford.

> And Wolf, without envy or spite,
> I know that you too, my frater,
> Easily overtop me now
> In all the decent qualities.
> > Wearing a white topee in Cairo,

Clapping your hands for "boys"
Under a creaking punkah in the embassy,
You are the young proconsul who
Keeps the burning world cool.
But what shall *I* do, Andrew,
What shall Abberville Minor
Do for his keep, for fifty years?
Oh but I've seen a dozen winking futures,
Thousands of beckoning vocations.
Tender and beloved healer:
Don immured in fragrant books
(Nights of sweet and solitary labour):
Undesisting womaniser:
Poet of new flowering in
Dead land and frosty silence.
Ever-wandering Jew or Sindbad:
Violent saviour at the kerb:
Grave rural eccentric:
Gilly in Sutherland, or else
A whaler in the wake of Ahab.
Or, in some green suburb of humility,
The Town Clerk. I'll be the Town Clerk!
    "Gavin! Laddy, but you played
    "A braw wee game on Saturday!"
    Oh my black Pict and wing-threequarter,
    Accelerating like an Alvis,
    Eluding fifty groping pairs
    Of Harlequin arms!
    Fellow of shining mystery,
    Gavin, if I could ever see
    Your naked Scottish soul I'd be
    Illuminatus for eternity.

And what would my black grandson say. . . .

    Grampa's old truculent face,
    Bearded like a LINCOLN imp

Or rough face of JESUS,
Seems as stony as this wall
I slap my hand against.
Yet old skins are crumbling faster
Than our own downy faces
Harden into hebetude.
  Tell me, christly Abraham,
  Would *you* stand, in our day,
  Behind the hungry barricades
  Of lean Wien—im Klösterreich?

What would my black grandson say for Lord Simon Snaith?
Shall I judge his brave brood by *that* sweet lord?
We all know it was Snaith who tarred and feathered Mercury,
And the shining boy a scrabby sight, at dawn over his pool.
But when the dean asks for the name of the boorish culpable
Does yon loutish lord own up and take his due?
Nay, no such nobleness obliges: comes, instead,
A certain lean, lop-sided sizor, giggling through his giglamps.
Such a black, ill-smelling serf as never had dared to show
His boils among the gaudy fools who frolic in Tom Quad.
  But eh, my louts, we're not such ninnies as you take us for:
  Not a ninny here but knows that Snaith had bribed the
  brute.
  And Lord knows which of the two I find the fouler fellow—
  The scrubby lordling or the cur who sold his brainright.

  Simon! Sluggish Simon! What shall we do? Where shall
  we go?
  To Parson's Pleasure first to watch Doctor Silenus
  Watching *us* with eyes like blue gobstoppers.
  And then? And after? Away in your Alvis, Simple Si,
  To *The Trout* or *The Rose Revived*, and by the sweet Thames
  To gargle a dry Moselle as the sun sets in the willows.
    And that ambiguous evasion by
    The purchase of a scapegoat at the price

Of six Jeroboams, or
Two dozen Coronas . . . well!
Who am I to raise an eyebrow, or
Purse these naturally pendant lips,
Or tap my fingers on a breviary.
"Let him cast the first stone . . ."

By golly, there's nothing worse than those lank, lurching idlers,
Oafs on horseback, idle squires and overgrown pages.
At least their fathers stiffened up their downy flesh to fight:
But in a sluggish peace these squirelings crack their whips at windows.

To forge the uncreated conscience of . . .
    "Loony! Loony Donovan!"
He was my fool
At the old school,
Of scabby pate
And lurching Irish gait.
But now my quondam loony,
James Augustus Donovan,
Virtuoso of the violoncello,
We are two glories of one brood and springing litter.
    Forge we together, James,
    Mother-murthering melodies.

Last night Lord Peter Pig did feast in the Garden Quad:
Pig-squeak in moonlight, and the brave ring of breakages.
Voices, I vow, full five notes shriller than a commoner's:
The shrill of a bagpipe sagging out its air upon the dusk.
    Adulteration of the blood! The thewed theigns have shrunk
    To adulterous dwarfs riding the wailing wives of dons to battle.

Attention there, Sir Bedevere!
Have a little faith in

A LEARNED CITY

The dying promise of the king,
Take the royal blade and hurl it far
Over the darkling waters of the mere.
  There the desert pants and shimmers;
  Here a mazy moonlight glimmers.
  Am I Abel's man or am I
  Still the son of ardent Mammy
  And her father's fevered, frantic
  Heir to all his moods romantic?
Well I do, I do wish
That I had a voice of my own, Matt—
As you often recommend, Matthew Miles.
And though I rage at homogeneous old men—
Monoliths;
Salt-flats;
Oak-trees—
I do, I do envy them
Their stern immutability.
  I'm horribly bothered at times, at night-times
  By certain imaginations of decay.
  Decay? I think I mean more the mixing
  Of something stinking in a noble head.

But as for you, my Ben-jamin—son of the right-hand—
Where are you giggling now, in a mock crown and tinsel robes?
His court shrinks, they tell me; a king of jacks and bob-tailed
fools:
A dance of mad dogs who wag their tails at Princey' belch.
  Ugh! Begone! I drain the filthy dregs of a sour wine:
  Of all filthy betrayals this was the most bitter. Filth!
  A mere tarnish on bright copper fattens into verdigris:
  Pus in the thumb fats and greens to gangrene the whole arm.
  Where dust lay faint as an eyelash in a boudoir of dead roses,
  Soon the room was rank and gassy with a dead duchess.
Two sons were lost to eye and ear: I buried both:
I sealed them up, my two sons, in the body of the boy Christian.

Behind the bratling's eye I saw the eyes of his blue brothers:
(They died on a line of field and blue: they fell into blue sky.)

> And I, an English lad of nineteen
> Blue and soaring summers, leaping falls,
> Cross an ancient, narrow lane,
> Change step to avoid
> Two perfumed shop-girls
> Agiggle, aglow in the mist.
> > And why does a twinge of memory cast up
> > A policeman dead on a dark bridge in Paris?

See how the stoat and the sick greyhound feed from the same trough!
Last week in hall did stoatish Abel dine Christian.
And wined him worthily, too, of our fame for tipplers and fruity topers:
Wined him until my son's face was a white fencing mask.

> I Dicko,
> Late of Wicklow,
> Wear the livery
> Of every company.

Patience, ye gods! Patience I need! Over the deathly floes . . .
Over the deathly floes and fields of the Jostedals brae . . .
Where was I climbing to? Or where falling? By golly!
Where did I . . . *Christian*! How he bore his dead brothers within him!
Up sheer Lofoten granite, out of the mouths of green wolves,
MY SON Christian climbed with neither ropes nor crampons.
Blue whale and Greenland seal as Kit clattered to the sky:
(Seven whiskered Wades did bellow out of a green sea.)
Blue whale and Greenland seal; puffin and kittiwake:
Uprose my son from grey granite into the blue air.
Christian climbed to the living blue—I in the boat below:
> (But *fallen*, had *fallen* his brothers, into the endless blue sky.)

He makes me to lather, Christian does,
Forever limpetting himself
To Simon, Roger, Mark and me.
  Whoa, Dickon Abberville,
  Scion of old Ramillies,
  Beside this deathly seminarist
  Upon whose Darwin-haunted face
  Acne bubbles like a hatch
  Of sedge upon an April river!
  How he *glares*, the aspirant,
  At all this frippery of
  A Gentleman's Outfitter:—
  Blue, electric pullover;
  Ties of fat, green corduroy;
  Riding-breeches, twill and leather;
  A cavernous Basque beret and
  Spats of violet brocade.
Dickon? Dicko? Ricky? Rick?
Accoutrement in a bright window
For twenty metamorphoses.
Which shall I be, shall I be
For you, Matt;
For you, Janet Carew, my lean love;
For you, Sir Abel, or for you
My glazed and faded uncle?
  Oh! Oh! What did I say of you!
  And what did I say of *you* beside me,
  All in cleric's grey!
  Forgive my beastly contempt,
  Rotten, beastly contempt!
Now I won't speak, I won't listen to
R. Abberville, a spiteful snob.

Back and knees! Back and knees! Like a silver spring
He rose in the chafing chimney, upward—back and knees—
skyward.

That was among the lakes of the Hardanger Vida; a summer's day:

The summer fjord was sucking at the thumbled rubble of the glacier.

Faltbot and black forearm on Sognefjord; and a blue sun:

Or up, four hundred feet, on Mjøsen Lake, where the sun faltered.

The black, unlustered lake was sunk a thousand feet below us:

A deathly shaft below, but white Christian dived from the rim.

In Lapland, too, on a lakeful of upside-down red rowan-trees;

A green Gunnar: the sap of the spruce sprang in Christian's branches.

> But, after the manner of poor Peer—Trog, vaer dig selv, nok!—
>
> Christian craved his buried trollhood, grinning upon the Glommen.
>
> Little troll, to thyself be enough! A giggling fool of the falls:
> Limp with a fool's laughter, lying low in the snickering shallows.

Was he *drunk*? But all we'd drunk was the gold and silver water.

Laughed he at *me*? Or at a troll who belched from the river's bottom?

But a clown, a coloured clown with rod dangling in the water:

I might have guessed this clown would never be the peer of Hendrik.

> A "social star"! A "people's choice"! How they *swooned* upon him!
>
> "Your boy is indeed a stellar apparition in these drab days."
>
> Beloved in Balliol where the melting dons adored my brazen "boy":
>
> Gold hair ablaze he shone in the dark stink of Belial.

And once I saw my "boy" through a window in Magdalen New Building:

The boyish cheeks were ruddled by a fever of Narcissus.

The *foulest* faces were raised to where he rose up in a corner of room:

A sick light was beamed on Peer from a fungus of monk-faces.

And it seemed as I watched that bosoms swelled on the boy's
hard chest:
His thighs bulged into womanly balloons; his bottom too.
Before his father's eyes Christian turned to a grossly witch:
His mien was of bright eyes popping from a bladder of milky
lard,
Farded by a brother-harlot; and the gaudy gibber of the
monks
Swelled him worse. I thought he'd burst with the loving milk
of monks.
The rich red of his raised glass sent to his darkling sire
A mocking ruby wink which said:—"*See* him, Hendrik's heir!"
    I moved back to the fellowship of softly-breathing fallow-
deer:
Beasts of the moon, breathe your sweetness on a soiled
brother.

      Unforgivably young I
      Change with every moon, or even
      Change in the twinkling of an eye,
      And must, as Rigorous Ricky enters,
      Interrogate the literal truth
      Of every metaphor or epitaph.
        Uncle Hendrik? Uncle Nils?
        Crystalised gold fruit, I say, of an old war,
        But in their living day what were they but . . .
      But no *debunking*, pray!
      How distinguish between
      The malice of belittlement
      And that cold eye I long to cast
      On all the features of the world?
        For oh Matt, I do, I do
        Admire the old brute, and yearn
        To share with you—and you so young!—
        The constancy of old men.
        But I'm the turncoat who

Laughs in pink, weeps in blue,
Wearing the gaudy livery
Of every passing company.

And then were all the living lights of the dead gathered
together:
I stole the light of their eyes as the dark waters filled them up.
I added light to the light I took from the bodies of the dead
lords,
And all these bequeathed lights did I in *Christian's* carcase
hang.

And yet my brother Andrew pines
For the battlefields he never trod,
The deaths he never died.
But I oppose the frivolity of these romantics,
Preferring to say,
With all you scrawny, banner-bearing marchers—
No more war!
Plus de guerre!
Nie wieder krieg!

The hearts of two sons cold with death: unnatural sons:
Me they mocked by taking early to the earth's cold comfort.
Filled with grief and age I shake to death in a cold house:
Cold! Cold! Cold! Yet boils are raised by the boiling blood.
I might have guessed Christian's doom when first he wooed
the witch:
Eh, that I'd but squeezed to mush her witchy white stem!

Oh my dark darling!
Oh my witch of Park Crescent!

Janet her name! And where did she spin her sticky threads
after?
Wove her web about Carew—this troll's jade; this Janet.

Lady of Sorrows! Lady of Situations!
  In Bagley Wood where bluebells shone
  Did Matthew Miles enlarge upon
  His friend's repellant vanity:
  He trembled for my sanity.
  "'Tis mad," he said "to boast about
  "Your lady's wicked ways, and shout
  "That never was a lady so
  "Woven on a web of woe."
Oh my celestial conscience!
Oh my sweet flautist and philosopher!

Aye, 'twas she who tapped the life of my green son:
'Twas that witch, more than any war, who brazed Bernard.

  My Uncle Christian's castaway,
  His draggled bird of yesterday.
  Not so much a bird as bat,
  Wings benighted, clawed and mat.
  I was thinking . . . I was saying . . .
  That oh, my dear, I *do* love
  Your delicate hysteria,
  Your sweet, keening dementia.

I knew that Christian would never be good for even a meanly
task
As soon as he took to the rocks and turned his back on the high
snow.
I saw him set out from the chalet with his three new fancy
friends:
The sheen of wind-proof jerkins; new boots of greased hide.
Crampons scraped the rock and axes swung like walking-
sticks:
Pitons winked from the pack, and the rope was a coil of silver
silk.

These "climbers" were crusted with gadgets as a crab with barnacles:
Spiders all beset with climbing-aids to scale a boulder.
They mounted a ladder of pitons. Oh danger! Ah horror!
Belayed above they climbed the face like lunch-time steeple-jacks.

JANET—there!
I didn't mean to let that name out.
Femme de Trente Ans—more than that—
And I her ingénu-initiate.
     She looks at me sometimes with *such* a look,
     As if I were nothing, too childish to be
     A *thing* at all. An ignorant little boy.
     I wish, I wish that I could be,
     A man of the wide world, not Perkin.
Warbeck?
At Exeter I ran away.
The whole of England laughed at me.

Thus, in the manner of the melted age, he chose the new and easy:
He turned his shameless shanks on the everlasting high snow
Of ridge and glacier, where the crevasse grins in the white deeps
And the wild white cornice hangs in the sky like a snow-hawk.
Our boy was *bored* by the white world—better liked the problems
Set by crack and chimney. Heh, it was a "problem child"!

"Morgen, Werner! Salut, Marc!"
(Pop-pop-popular Dick!)
But both sniffed at her door once:
The dirty dogs to sniff and paw!
     But child, child, keep your mind away

30

A LEARNED CITY

From that celestial boudoir where the world
Contracts into a cube of musk and blue
To keep the lady and her boy
Safe from the dark disturbance of the spring.
("The dark disturbance . . ." No, no it's only
Another rotten, plagiaristic echo of
The Master of the Drowned Phoenician Sailor.)

I do forswear the fruit of my loins; and of their loins:
Christian's slack seed and all the addled eggs of Gulveig.

A prince of the sun he laughed in his red and white
Bugatti,
Waving—with her! with her!—on the green road from
the farm
As he left for the hot seas. Merman! God of the Wind!

And even the son of my choice is only a dry, disabled man:
Even Carew can never breed: or the green wife is barren.
My rising heart! I should have been a stem and an old
trunk:
I should have been the Abram of an old stone race.

A Lear of dark autumnal college gardens:
Monstre Sacré. Moloch of the North.
A barren patriarch, he ruled a race
Of old stone men on Iceland's shore.
But oh Uncle Christian, damn it, damn it all,
Where did you lose your godly head?
What have you done with your youth?
When did you eat your future up,
Uncle Christian?
In youth not bestial,
Bright, celestial,
He ordered his friends

To make amends.
Janet, David, Edwardo
Lost their bravado,
Were made to apologise
By Christian, Prince of the Sunrise.
   And should she fall
   Into abstraction
   Still dreams of the tall
   Lost lover and his subtraction.
Oh Uncle Christian, damn it all!
A young Poseidon running on the dunes
Of windy Norfolk. Eheu Norah Otway!
Eheu sinking sun and prince
Of my benighted lady!

Nights are brewed in beds of seed and sweat. What a mixing!
Would that Thor could turn his heel on such adulterous
coupling!
   Spar! Spar on the chimney piece! Old salted wood:
   Grey wood smoothed by the tongues of fifty thousand tides.
   Ships burned on a strange shore, and Norway far to the
south:
   They warmed their hands at a pyre of salt ships burning
blue.
   And then these newcomers led their sick horses from the
shore:
   Tarry hands slapped at rumps on the dunes of Svinafell.
   By break of day all the men were mounted and riding inland:
   By the first snow each had ploughed a furrow around his
fell.
The fell kingdoms! A kingdom is anywhere a man freely moves:
Wherever a man moves of his own will, there he reigns.

   But everyone remembers how
   He could twirl and bend and straighten,
   Taking a low pass, stooping,

Half falling just to fool them,
Dancing, *lolling* through the lurching
Hounds of Cambridge breaking from the pack.

"Njal said to Bergthora, 'Now our bed awaits us:
" 'Let us lie down together before the beams fall down.'
"So they lay together, Njal and his wife, under a fresh fleece,
"And the room below roared as the red wind blew the walls.
" 'So are we soothed to sleep,' said Njal, lying beside his wife.
" 'We shall not fear freezing now.' And as he spoke the beams
"Broke under the bed, and the bed burned as it fell down."

And all who burned there, or fell at the farm door,
Entered the grey kingdom of the sleepers.
   Fishing in Lethe,
   (Sleepy chub under the grey banks.)
   Fishing in the sour waters of Styx,
   (Lampreys glow in the deeps:
   A hieroglyphic pike intrudes
   His sullen snout.)
Sniff the river-wafting air that blows
Around this eloquent parabola.
Barley-sticks of Mary's porch;
The hunched shoulders of inbred All Souls;
A queenly cupola and choiring tower—
All the renowned curve across the heart
Of the celestial city.
   Our little famous, infamous grey town!

And how they howled outside; screeched and capered; *trembled* at last:
Whimpered at last—Flosi and his fellows—to see the burning of Njal.
   Fellows! In what cold college are *burners* taught their trade—Flosi, Grani and Glum; Kol and Ozur and the sons of Sigfuss?

I mean—this pack recalls—such fellows as Wade, Hodgett
and Bliss:
A filthy fellowship. Oh, Flosi was too good for such fellows!
No one, in Njal's day, fed his brain to a sick fatness
As Bliss crams his crop with the fattened livers of sick geese.

Oh Royal Rumania, sweeten my path and may I follow
    your epaulettes into the golden shades of Sybaris!
Oh Brown Bomber, fight for all whose lips are ripe and
    stained purple, and for all whose eyes are soft with
    gospel truth!
Oh Queen Christina, sink your frosty eyelash over me
    and may I live in the zebra-shadows of those hairs!
Oh Kingfish of Louisiana, may I hook you hard in the
    horny gullet of your lies, and play you all night in
    the hot gulf before I gaff you!
Oh Fat Freebooter and Gross Aeronaut, your horrible
    fat shall be rendered down at last in grief and vain
    repentance!
Oh Edward Albert Christian George Andrew David,
    droop from the throne with the dark-scallopped
    eyes of a boy-wastrel, and carry all our abdications
    on the shoulders of your raglan overcoat!
Oh Vicar of Stiffkey, be for us all the avenging clown of
    the soiled cloth. Oh our Diogenes!

I who dug for the buried saws and kennings of the poor:
I who found a living folk behind a gilded Siegfried.
    "Better a home, though hovel it be: a man is master at home:
    "Though wattled his house, his herd lean, better it be than
    begging."
"Filled and fed let farmer ride, though his garments gape:
"Never blush for breek or boot: feed the belly first."
    A dry and stony folk, they saw no heaven above the sky:
    None sought further than the frosty ground and the salt sea.

I have desired to go,
Above all heavens,
To the miraculous white city of New York
Where the sky-high rich dine on their icy pinnacles.
A muted negro,
In white jacket and bow-tie,
Pouts his purple lips on a silver trumpet-teat
And blows in time to the distant hooting of the Aquitania.
    Absurd illusion!
    Childish and meretricious fantasy!
    (Or so your eyebrows tell me, Matt, as I make them rise,
    I see them raised high above your blue Picasso.)

And now, when the lean levellers screech to bring us all low,
Honour Iceland, where each farmer was king of his own kin.
A world where honour was paid to each rank and every calling:
A world where no man was to another a gibbering animal.
    (The groom at Bulmer's place, whose skin was grained with stable-dust,
    Stall-fellow of fat cob, gelding and rangy colt,—
    More horse than man was he to the eyes and noses of his betters.
    And those betters, passing above with beaks and muzzles high,
    Were neighing unicorns to him, and gabbling yellow griffins.)

    ("Neighing unicorns!" he neighed:
    And what's the Prof to me
    But an engravéd beast
    In an ancient bestiary.)

Thverfell! Thence to Skorrodale and the grey Sulur Hills:
Thence he rode to Akratongue, to Berjaness and Keldur.
And Hoskuld's mother was called Thorgerd, daughter of Red Thorstein:

And Red was the son of Olaf the White, son of Helgi and
Thora,
Son of Ragnor Hairy-Breeks, daughter of Sigmund Snake-
heart.
   Ah, the thrumbling names of Iceland, how they kindle me!

    Above the florid casket red roses swell
    Like a suffusion of the dead mobster's chest,
    A last kindling of his hot sicilian heart.
    Behind him, decorous as deacons in the limousines,
    His gunmen ride with flanks swollen by their holsters
    And scarred faces strained to a grieving rigidity.
    And on the side-walk, in the lake-side public-gardens,
    The mayor, the chief of police, the local cardinal
    Bare and bow their heads to the passing of Tomaseo.
       A violent innocence I thought . . . "Hiya, Sam!"
       My lean lincolnian friend, prophet from Idaho,
       Salutes at Canterbury Gate with hairy fingers.
       No scholar's gown can tame this rough economist:
       He walks like a rolling sailor of the billowed prairies,
       A pistol slapped on each thigh—this way, that way.
       Our junior—clumsy child of the innocent blue wilds:
       Our senior—mute, sober and sly as we play the fool.
       Who, on these ancient parapets, will ever know you?

None ever cried, like the yelping Greek, against his darkest
doom:
None ever tried to bargain with the sun, or to beat down the
wind.

    Grampa excoriates "the Modern Age";
    Regrets that Christ has conquered the god Thor;
    Yet still would ring poetic lilies
    Out of the darkened sun at Ragnarok
    Or Helgi dead, beloved by Hogni's daughter.

But, Fortunatus, I shall always be
The infant of my century.
And therefore with a westward eye
I watch upon the western sky
The star of Ginger rise and die,
Dancing with her partner wry.
And over there, a shameless star,
The prowler with the gross cigar
And black, concupiscent moustache
Mixes love with love of cash.
Oh my America, my Nova Zemlya!
Oh my New-Found-Land!
Groucho is Lincoln's heir:
Astaire dances in the wake
Of Sherman, that incendiarist.

In Helgi's tomb Sigrun said: "Now I know my lord:
"Happy am I as Odin's hawk, wet with dew at dawn.
"Now I delight in Helgi dead, as Odin's haggards hover:
"As hungry hawks rejoice, sighting a dying beast in the bush.
"Helgi, your hair is thick with rime and cold with the dew of
death:
"Chill are your cheeks. How shall I give you peace, my dead
prince?"
(Aye! Aye! They were tender too, and in song artful.)
"Dear daughter of a dead foe, I must leave you lying.
"For I must ride the reddening ways before the cock crows:
"I must spur my foaming horse high over cliffs of cloud.
"For the dead must be west of Windhelm Bridge before the
yellow sun
"Winks on Hogni's dark hill and wakes the warrior host."

Or, to put it more obscurely,
Father Abraham, it seems,
Fathered Sweeney's waking dreams
Of Doris in the bloody wood
And Dusty in red riding hood.

So they sang and told their tales until the year a Thousand:
Year of the grubs who rolled ashore in clanging fumes of
incense.
Came to our coast men we took first for fat, grey women:
Folded in fat cloth they tripped and tumbled, climbing the
beach.
And one of them set in a grey dune a stained silver cross;
And on the cross a mannikin had stretched his creaking arms.
We shivered to see the black imp buckled on our shore:
And the southern rain sighed on the shore, the soft rain of
Ireland.
   And then the great worm rose and wailed against the wind:
   Oh that the wind had blown his wailing back to holy
   Ireland!
   "Pater Noster Qui . . ." A spiced tongue of the rotten South:
   A rotting stink is borne on the bloodied winds of old Iceland.
And then did the droning grubs wriggle north through all the
land:
And then were all the sagas sugared by that sweet blood.
Now were the old songs heard no more in the high halls:
And now was Asgard struck to a gallery of stone gods.
And so they stood, or knelt, or bowed, till the sun went down:
And Baldur's fallen body was not so dead as these stones.
Stony-still with grief they grieved, too, for their own passing:
For none but guessed at last that even the gods must pass away.
   Thus they grieved till Odin heaved his heavy shoulders up:
   His sobs burst like a thunder-storm that breaks a long frost.

   So I grieved in the Camera
   For Dick the humpen boar who fell
   With bloody tusks on Bosworth field.
      "Amaze the welkin with your broken staves!"
      And bearing his own villainy
      As well as all that decadent
      And monstrous armour of the age,
      He fought for a dark and dead cause
      With a devilish panache.

38

On the other hand it can easily be maintained
That the victor became one of our greatest kings.
Above all he managed to *economise*;
Putting an end to the evils of alienation
By means of a vigorous campaign of resumption;
Selling knighthoods at a higher rate;
Improving the annual yield of tunnage and poundage:
Diverting cash from the antiquated Exchequor
Into the new office of the King's Chamber:—
In short, he made the royal treasury
Not only solvent, but rich and independent.
    Well sir, there it is—the usual choice:
    Romantic Satan laughing into Hell,
    Or that cheese-paring, sober-sided Lord
    Who set to rights th'economy of Heaven.

"I know that I hung on the windy tree nine nights long:
"Spiked with a spear, to Odin given: Odin given to Odin.
"There I gathered the runes of grief and sang them into the
wind:
"Tree-tossed Odin sings in the snow as the wolf swallows the
sun."

    "Ha, Simon! *Dear* Roger!"
    (Pink nobs in Tom:
    Crystalline quad of blazing snow
    Where frozen water-lilies glint
    Under a lewd Mercury.)
    "See you chez Bliss tomorrow morning."
       (And Bliss purring, last week:—"The time which he—
       "The time which he can spare from—
       "From the adornment of his person he—
       "He devotes—he devotes—
       "To the neglect of his duties.")

Horn of Elkland on the wall! Long, long since
You blared your frozen cry over the reedy lakes of Finmark.

A plague of boils; and slack muscles yaw in the calf like sails
Unwinded in the north fjord. By golly, the damned years!
And the tall room no longer mine, where the old sea-trophies
Hang on the pale walls. Eh, my lads of Kristiania!
But why should an old fool lust after his young years?
The years are filled behind me; and all the shadows had their
say.
Horn on the southern wall, be silent now forever after!
Who, by blowing you, could raise the silent years again?

But how he makes me yearn, love,
For somewhere somewhat further *south*,
Where dusky dulcimers are plied
Under the banana's shade.
  Fare further, Lord Odysseus!
  Wheel your ship 'twixt Abyla and Calpe:
  Sail, sail beyond the farthest gaze of Alexander
  And munch in the far South-East
  The mandarins of wisdom.
Why did they always steer my childish eyes
To the cold wastes of beastly Boreas?

As in this pure and early light of my flemish master,
No early light so clear to me as dawn light on the fjord.

Names dug in stone, and gilded: flaking gilt:
Aureate names of the dead, as monumental now
As any hieroglyph on sphynx or pyramid.
  (Land of Tutankhamon; land of the dead!
  But Wolf, amid those vast deathly persuasions,
  Be absolute for life, with the palm and the tamarisk.)
Simon, my pal from pale palladian palaces,
Will never do as his five stone uncles did—
Swap the fullness of his days for gold letters.

A LEARNED CITY

A bustling west wind had scooped the fjord into scallop-shells,
And a red side of salmon twisted down the windy street.

> But pop-pop-popular Dick
> Sniffs the wind, runs as quick,
> Under arches, over grass,
> As bunny with the bob-tailed arse.
> Libera Nos a malo!
> But why, as I run, does the memory shout within
> Of a policeman dead on a dark bridge in Paris?
> Oh but I run to escape
> The war-memorial in the porch,
> The skull, the pyramid
> And the soft shade of a dead man
> Under the windy taffrail of a bridge.
> Must I think on't? Nay rather,
> Breathing sweetly now, I run
> Under Ruskin's yellow hideosity
> And out, *out* to the snowy wastes of Meadows.
> Libera Nos a Malo!

And still I see the salmon-face of the chasing fishmonger:
And still the fish-kite is twirled and trundled by the wind.
And you—Møller! Brøndrum! Sjørvik! Hølm! Erikson!—
You, the Moose; the Saint; the Dog and Baby; Finmark Fiend.
Boys I loved or hated long ago; and naught between
Loving and hating, then. Eh for the days of ice and fire!

> Now *I* prefer the emerald boys
> Of Twenty-Three to Grampa's brood
> Of yellow Siegfrieds on the fjord.
> And *you* above them all,
> Baby-face in a fur coat,
> With megaphone uplifted—*there*!—
> From the dingy gothic sill
> Booming over grass and kine:—

"Ap-ril is the cru-el-est month".
And all the great bemuscled oarsmen,
Scarfed Christs bearing their crosses,
Turned and flushed and laid their crosses down.
  Would that I'd been there, Matt,
  To join th'embattled aesthete there
  And hurl the clattering oarsmen down the stair!
  But, "I fear," my gentle Conscience answers,
  "You'd have contrived instead
  "Some shocking camaraderie of clownish charm;
  "Wearing, as you must, the livery
  "Of every iridescent company."
(But I have heard them, too, the ancient beasts,
Cursing from the tops of stairs
As Abberville's dirty feet
Rattle the worn stairs,
  Libera Nos a Malo!)

And all in our glazed caps, bright-coloured for each class,
We seethed about the Storting: brazen boys with yellow hair.

  How they seethe in ardent causes,
  "Bernard's" growling Bolshevics,
  Drunk with alcoholic
  Politics!
    (But after our last alacrity
    In international perfidy
    Bliss delivered *this* to the company:—
    "Our heads, I take it, are bowed but unbloody.")

Many a brave bark for Sverdrup's bright and singing sword:
Many a howl for Oscar in his Swedish water-palace.
All the flags and cracked cries again of Forty-Eight:
"FRIHET! BRORSKAP!" Crying for a future in a past.
  And how we roared on the windy streets as Nansen rode by:
  A young face burned black across the Greenland ice.

All, we *all* long to see
The undeniable hero passing by,
Standing alone in a chariot of red roses.
His eyes see nothing of the shouting street;
His face is frozen by the recollection
Of all that lay *behind* his gallant past.
And yet his cold, marmoreal figure-head
Cleaves that whistling future up the street
Where rain is scudding off the fish-quay.
    (Such a one, for my Ovidian queen,
    Would be an intellectual knight of love,
    A tireless student of the amorous lore,
    Precise in all his nice and courtly moves
    And erudite in feigned adultery.
    God help me, Matt, but if I hear another word about
    the Doctor Egregius I shall either go bonkers or take
    my knife to the queen.

'Tis there, there on the wall, the snow-blackened face of
Fridtjof!
And as he rode the street we too had crossed the snows of
Greenland.
Our Fridtjof, calm as the North; silent master of Thule:
The sagas throbbed to life again, after a vile age.

    I couldn't for the life of me resist
    The temptation to make fun
    Of Nielson, Saga-sage and Master;
    Worshipper of all past ages;
    Idolater of earliest things.
    Said I bewailed the passing of the "very first" dynasty,
    Of which the rest had been but "pale travesties".
    And I went too far—dear, but I went too far!—
    Blowing my nose hard to hide manly tears,
    With "Ah, my sweet, first Pharaoh—buried prince!"
    And "Ah, my pristine, unicellular mavourneen!"

But he hates clowning and buffoonery
(As I do too: I hate it too!)
And he hates impertinent young men.
He flushed: I stammered:
He turned his back: I shuffled my feet.
Nothing to be proud of there.
Nothing for self-congratulation there.

And at the midsummer of that year Erikson and I
Fought at midnight in a sunny glade of northern Finmark.
I fought Erikson under the midnight sun, and left him lying:
He lay and blubbered with his face deep in the sponge of the
wet moss.
For I won't allow a dirty sleery tale from anyone:
Why should I hear the holy forest fouled by his beastly boast-
ing!
Climbing from Oslo northward, how the pole was piled
above us!
Climbed the frozen dome of the world to that imagined
steeple.
Deaf are these mountains: blind are they, and of men
meagre:
Even the rafts of logs are unmanned on grey Glommen.

Sir Pockly Dick of portly mien,
His nose a bursting grape of Douro,
Rode into a forest green
A-searching for a cure-oh.

But there my lady Gonorrhoea,
Dripping mucus from her ——,
Filled the woodland folk with fear
On her cockle-hunt.

And Syphilis the shepherd, he,
Singer of arcadian roses,
Moans a sylvan elegy
For our faithless noses.

A LEARNED CITY

Pocked are ash and oak and elm;
Turtle-doves are black with crabs.
On a wheezing chanterelle
A squirrel picks his scabs.

Mouse and badger, fox and deer
Miscegenate with furry gusto.
There the tumid fungi rear,
Purple-high with lust-oh.

But now the fungus climbs until
Sky and phallus seem to meet;
And all adown old Bollock Hill
Rolls the spirochaete.

We mix historical ages up which time has kept asunder:
Historians' dirty fingers foul the clear dream-waters.
Rooting like swine in the clear and balmy forests of our youth
We dig up dirty truffles there; adulterate the dream.
  But now I'll tell you, Bernard, the old boys of Ninety-Five,
  The senior fellows of my first year, *they* were such men as knew
  How to flay, with scarcely a flexed elbow, any "Pastor" Bannion;
  Any swollen shaver, cub, or cheeky greenhorn.
  Demon GILES, who cracked Etruscan tombs like cockle-shells:
  BRAGG's scooping eye, raising a sunken truth from the page.
  Ungodly grandees, the last lingerers from war in heaven:
  They'd stormed high heaven and found it empty of good angels.

  But I, being an English youth,
  Of twenty soaring summers . . . Wait!
    I shall be that quiet poet who
    Lives in a white house by a rocky sea
    And once a day is seen from the far cliff
    Strolling among his salty garden gods.

And there—*gaze, gaze* upon Slouch shambling kitchenward!
A scout of the new breed; fag adangle from a slobbered lip.
   Tombes, my friend! Old Frederick Tombes of the white and
   burnished beaver:
   The green-baized breakfast tray, and Frederick's soft
   "Good-day".
   He swung the curtains back on a new century of falling
   snow:
   A conjuror, he pulled the cloth to show a feast of silver.
The buried are out of sight, and few have held them hard in
the mind:
I am the spokesman and remembrancer of heavenly hosts.
Let no dark dirges . . .

     "Let no dark dirges moan, though I must fare far."
     "Yet would I wage wrathy war against the man who
       mocked
     "Your lingered lays and all the songs you sang on
       Iceland's shore."
      (Cries the buffoon who wears the livery
      Even of Nielson's company.)

Aye, they mock and sneer my verses. Stink of snakes, I curse
The cobblers of the city verses; church and charnel-house . . .

   Well! I never in the world meant—Mama Mia!—
   To raise his bristles so and make him snort aloud.
     Dear Simon, it was too shy-making for words:
     Oh Chris, I blushed to my ears and the roots of my
     hair:
     Darling, I couldn't have longed more for the earth to
     swallow me.

But *they* were never cursed with the sickness of "self-examina-
tion":
Narcissus never swooned at his own face on the fells of Thule.

A LEARNED CITY

Unlike—I know what follows—introspective *us*,
Darling one, whose minds are like a honeycomb
By *ourselves*—by Dick and Janet—bored and *bored*.
Effete epigones, I fear; for short, pigs.
    De plus, si j'ose le dire, dear, I stand before him
    In a most nauseous and debilitated opposition
    To Njal, the farmer-sage, and all his men of yore.
    (Yore! Yore! The Prof's only true love.)

A youth sailed from the North-West, legs astride the dragon:
The youthful Viking rode, and the oaken dragon drank the
sea.
Came, a youth, to the misty shore, and oars squealed in the
tholes:
Thor be with us! There he glooms, the Count of the Saxon
Shore.
Suddenly, high on the green shore of England, what a giant!
Colossal RHODES in the morning mist, wearing a pith helmet.
    From Harwich, yes, I came in a blue train to the capital:
    Imperial days! A colonel on the quay in white drill.
    And talk of Zulus in the other train that stopped to pant
    While over the roofs the spires slept in the sun of a dying
    century.
    It *shall* be shone through all the stinking dark of Africa.

    "My heart belongs to Daddy" Michael sadly sings,
    Still sweaty from the Grind, in stained white breeches,
    Sitting on the worn step of Peckwater Number Three.
        And "Daddy, let me stay out late" was Nell's moan
        In the moon, in the moon of Magdalen's gaudy ball.
        (So many Fathers invoked by us grieving orphans.)

Three hours I walked the city ere I came to Merton:
I saw my long shadow sweep the summer flank of Christ
Church.
I heard the bells clatter in twenty towers, and saw the dome

Of the Camera gleam in the late sun; and saw Benjamin
Jowett.

> Where shall we go? We'll go this Sunday morn to Wood-
> stock,
> Drink with His Grace of Blenheim, victor of Ramillies,
> Our Captain-General for a summer's day.
>> But I, being an English youth
>> Of twenty sharp and stirring winters,
>> Take to my toes again and run
>> Out of that rancid summer where
>> I spoke with the yellow-pollened tongue
>> Of a foetid tiger-lily.

And when this Norseman stuck his burning beard through
Merton gate
The giant Bragg laid his heavy arm along my back.
Etruscan Giles, with eyes like opened tombs—a buried sun—
Shone his buried Oxford light on my barbaric beaver.
In Mob Quad the oak-and-leather cell of the great Bragg
Was steeped in the male breath of wood-smoke and anchovy.

> Come, what is he, barbarous Abberville?
> A demi-English youth who
> Was born in the month of Sarajevo,
> Blessed with a stout and limber frame,
> Partial to the tang of smoked fish,
> An intimate of Matthew Miles. . . .
>> But a damned chameleon, a damned
>> Man of putty under the thumb
>> Of every Oxford button-moulder.

GORRINGE, ghostly philosopher! Prophet of the Absolute!
Sailor in heaven's blue, snuff and sleep you dearly loved.
In the Fellows' Garden Gorringe sneezed in the deeps of a
deck-chair:
His ghost winged into deep heaven—and back in time for tea.

A LEARNED CITY

Arcus Senilis rising over
Nielson's blue and godless eye.
(But one day I may be
Of *Christ's* company.)
 And may I never, Baldur God of Youth,
 Possessed by envy and forgetfulness,
 Rage at the "younger generation",
 Or weep for the time-enchanted ghosts
 Of commonplace, forgotten men.
Oh Your Senility,
Ancient Richard, pray die in humility!
Today only dirty old men
Flatter the young, and then
Make their passes,
Defunct fingers tittering at our arses.

All had fought against the king in the late wars of religion:
Bragg and Giles had won their spurs against the Gallows King.
But all were of a rich mind and a faith that bloomed in the sky.
All, in Meadows or in Mesopotamia, saw The Leaf
Above the thousand rattling leaves of oak and sycamore.
Plato's sons were we again, and mindful of The One.
Oxford lay in a dream of seers, until those fenland frauds,
Scrawny netherlandish scavengers were heard here.
The Mathematico-How-D'you-Say! The Meaning of a Mean-
ing!
As if a meaning lay in cutting the One into twenty parts!
 Aye, but these dry sappers of the Cam could mine and melt
 All our dreams; all our laws . . .
 Until our cripples shall be cuckolded by any beardless brat.

 By what law, old shipmate, in what dream,
 Did vast Leviathan in osiers rot
 And thoughtful dead men drift down bubbling seas?
 Only the poet makes his dream a law
 And rules the world by dreaming out its laws.

So to the golden youth
I proclaimed the truth,—
He was the *only* poet,
Did they but know it.
Meet to receive
Le Bateau Ivre,
Read, *read* him, Simon!
Never say die, man!
Chris the flocculent,
Cuddly and opulent,
Pray drive us gently
In your Rolls Bentley
Down the hill to Henley.
After the ball
And the lisping, tall
Debutantes,
Who wants
To be back in college
When all the foliage
Of early morning
Quakes to our roaring?
See how the swan's daughter
Beats, doubled on air and water,
Up this river-avenue.
And somnolent Gavin, you
Never will wake in time
For the alpine climb
Through the new-fanglement
Of spikes and barbed-wire entanglement.
How shall we save your bacon,
Oh you forsaken,
Benighted sot
And bestial Scot?

And I was of those later Northmen, too, who sailed the seas
And colonised the dark. We fought to lighten the dark
South . . .

Old   *Aye, now he'll be off upon his dream of Empire.*
Abberville   *(None but a foreigner, I thought,*
             Could ever have made so bright a rainbow image
  Of what to an Englishman was mere prerogative,
  Or merely the business of living.)
    So weightily *he moves from topic to topic,*
    From one grouse to the next,
    And ever in the tramp of his seven stresses,
    Saxon in speech,
    Ponderous in alliteration;
    An old giant tramping the fells of Iceland.
  Why yes, an old monster, too, without a doubt,
  Barbarous in the violence of his visions,
  Loving, perhaps, not even himself, still less
  The living son or daughter.
  And yet for Bernard Carew he must have felt
  An itch, *at least, of lost paternal affection,*
  And bitterly he did bewail his Bernard's cuckolding.
    Now, as his rage rises,
    You'll hear him damn the careless youth
    First for the crime of his love-affair
    With Janet, that poor witch of meagre love,
    And then for his greater crime in leaving her.
    But as for me—no partisan of either.
    I find his heavy pace a comfort now,
    And even his arid rages pardonable;
    Whereas the darting flights of the youth—
    A hectic dragon-fly above the violent river of his life—
    Troubles my eye as I try to follow him,
    Exhausts my patience by his inconsequence.
    (He was not of your breed, dear boy,
    Nor ever would have spent his fishing days
    Attending to an old man's falsifying memory.)
  Yet hope he had, at least, that heady virtue;
  Shame for his grosser faults;
  Self-ridicule;
  An eye alert for every colour and shape of the world;

And if perverse, why polymorphously,
Wearing his five and thirty liveries
With a devilish panache.
  Strangely my sympathies divide and falter
  Between the elderly and rutted foe,
  My terrible old Grampa, and
  This youth who made me what I am,
  This brash accomplice of a many-coloured age.
  Hear them further, Olaf;
  Hear them out;
  Be warned by both.

Wauchope wallowed in his own blood. At Magersfontein:
And as I held him up his arm-pits burst with warm blood.
The while I saw stars shoot and the rocks turn red:
The night was torn in two: the sky thundered and fell down.
  But by golly, those boys never *squeaked* in battle!
  You there—Pigsqueak—Pipsqueak below, who squealed
away an Empire!

  Basso Profundo, I ABBERVILLE!
  (BERVILLE! Berville! berville! ville!)
  Yet did so shrink away, the name—
  Diminu . . . . end-Oh!—
  In a wood of moss and terror
  Over the valley of the mausoleum.
    Yet am I of that European heritage,
    Of Palomède's cousinage,
    Even in stony death to lie
    Unechoed where the echoes die.
  Art a page, then, in the court of true love?
  Do'st serve thy lady as thy noble sires before thee?
    Nay sirrah, God forbid I serve her so!
    I am not so commanded to my courtesy
    But ever a humble squire, and so shall stay.
    Sometimes, perhaps, even he of the motley,
    He of the cap and bells.

Clowns in the quad below, who squeak. . . .
Brother Boers, dead on the dusty hill; grave goodmen:
Bearded farmers; worthy foes; men of the misted earth.
They served as Njal's men or Gunnar's freely served their
feres:
They chose their own chiefs, nor ever touched their hats to 'em.
  But ever I loved one dream better than the best of fellows:
  I dreamed of lordship bowed in service over Africa.
  A farmer's boy beside the fjord slept on a cold shore
  And dreamed of that old god who carried fire to darkened
  men.
  They dream today of blood-red beggars riding through our
  houses,
  But I of the young theigns shining on a dark continent.

     Swans ruffle and swell:
     A dog lifts his leg
     And pocks the snow with yellow.

        Icy shore of Isis:
        Fresh paint of winter barges:
        Clenched willow-trees.

     Swans swell on Isis:
     Pocked snow:
     Mrs Bannion's cheeks are like moss-roses.

        Icy Mrs Bannion, Swan of Isis,
        Lift your leg
        And pock the snow.

     Lady, river and bird,
     Soon I'll fly
     Far from all these painted barges.

        Snow lady,
        River Isis,
        I must leave you for the Queen of Egypt.

     Oh, the ancient nursery shame!
     Oh, desire that crumbles all respect!

Oh, castles of shame and seasons of disrespect!
   Better to be full-throated in disrespect.
Cripes, but she did
Etwas malodorous in the linen-cupboard.
    "Cats on the roof-tops," ...... *frankly* ecstatic:
    "Cats on the tiles," .... *overt* in sexuality:
    "Cats with syphilis," .... bearing the wounds of
                      love:
    "Cats with piles," .... and ridicule:
    "Cats with their ARSE-holes ... in diction unashamed:
    "*Wreathed* in smiles," .... in mien exultant:
    "Revelling in the joys of copulation." ... Which I
      greatly prefer to *your* sly innuendoes, oh World, oh
      Grandfather. And also to the courtly claptrap of
      my divine mistress.

But *we* followed the northern light, over the Orange River,
Across green Limpopo and up to the raging white Zambesi,
And northward up the Congo; north and east to the Nile's
rising;
Northward, northward, bringing light to all the steamy rivers.

   But I in an enseaméd bed,
   In steamy-scented sheets have known
   Unspeakable contrivances.
     But if I could say NO, without offence ...
     Her arms and legs are wet as water-snakes ...
   But ha, my boy, and ah, my lad,
   Who can measure the deep and dreadful blight
   Of dread *Repression*? What if the tall Agrippa of dreams,
   The dark nocturnal censor, were to walk
   Across the *waking* day!

Colonel Jake! Fiery Jake of Magersfontein!
The bearded doctor doused your eye of all its fighting fires.

The fiery heart of a fighter was softened on a doctor's couch;
Opened up to the quizzing eye; folded in wet flannel;
Gently doused until, with a stink and a sputter of greasy
smoke,
The flame failed and the fatty heart dripped in a bland
chest,
The reeking, red-blue eyes, which had burned up six
squadrons,
Sopped to a muddy marsh-brown, doggy with gold-sparks.
The bone-hard ram's head had risen into plump dough:
The icy mouth had blubbered out into loose pink lips.
The cured colonel walked in the park with five fat dachshunds:
His cured and faded eye blinked across the Serpentine.

 Oh but I rather fancy the new Trinity
 Of Ego and wild Id, and God the Super-Ego
 Frowning aloft, or raising shocked palms to the sky.
  I've often thought that Wolf is the very best type
  Of Freudian man, whose Id fumes in the chest
  Like sullen Etna in the dizzy air of Sicily.
  Or sometimes Andrew's servile Caliban would wink
  From under the cold lash and all-seeing eye
  Of Prospero, his diplomatic Super-Ego.
 (Deborah? Deborah?
 Who could believe in her?)

Wauchope wallowed in his own blood. At Magersfontein:
And as I held him up his arm-pits burst with sticky blood.
  Eh, let us burn these reeky jungles down, and bring the light
  Of Oxford streams to every sweaty Caliban of the night!

 Out of my mind, old chap! Three laughing girls!
 The Fisher-King's daughters dancing by.
 Oh to lay me down in the shade of girls in bloom!
  They pass me on the river side; and did I swerve
  To put them nearer to the leechy bank, and so
  To make them symbols of the womby waters?

55

Or did I, swaying to the uddered cows of Meadows,
Shrink away from all that frisky heiffer-love
And totter back to Mummy's milky domes?
And a strange bewilderment it is, Matthew Miles,
To feel on every lightest thought or motion of the body
A hundred crafty meanings crouch in strange devices.
Griffins and unicorns cavort
In lecture-hall and library,
And in each privy of the flesh
The rod of love may bud.
 Bliss murmuring of Rodney Hanged:—
 "Doesn't one rather feel that Rodney's death
 "Has taken the gilt, taken the gilt off
 "The gingerbread of suicide?"
But rather, but rather
Death is the only gilder.
Dickon the Boar's hump
Shines golden after Bosworth.
Not all the economies of the seventh Harry,
Perkin's cold murderer,
Can rub the sullen bloom
From off that hump of gilded gingerbread.
 See how it rises, scaled with green gold,
 The weedy hump of Carp-Leviathan,
 Out of the suds of Emma's washing-tub.
 And at the very sight of it
 Emma's privy parts do bud
 With golden-rod, with golden-rod.
 And all about this brazen dome—
 Or breast of mermaid, copper-green—
 Bubbles wink and swim like eyes;
 Eyes that burst in tears and birds.
  A yellow eyelash splashed
  And sank a clipper in the port of Stockholm.

And the crooked paths would be straight; terror would cry
and die in the light:

Trees would be felled for the sun to fall on steaming night-soil.
Little wrinkled men; pygmies smeared with blood and filth—
To bring them light, and grow them tall in the white light of
the sun.

    Three nights running have I stood alone,
    Bathed in a moon-reflecting sweat,
    Atop a single battlement
    Of our rugged and heroic bell-tower.
      I mean—knowing I have a rotten head for heights
      I simply *had* to conquer the ghastly pinnacle.
      For *her* sake, however ludicrous that may seem.
    Oh but I read you, Matt, my shrewd old freudian freund!
    Yes, yes! The phallus my objective, ohne Zweifel.
    And I, as ever, seeking a simply divine erection.
      Or was it the fear of falling
      Deep, deep into the appalling
      Pouch, womb or velvet tummy
      Of my hollow, howling Mummy?

We battered down the damned mimosa in the spiked darkness,
And ever ploughed our dusty boots towards the hill of hell.

    And does the heart of the youth rise a little higher
    To see, new-painted on the poop of his college barge,
    His college arms embossed in argent, gules and azure?
    Nay sirrah, not so. (Though I do admit
    To an absurd partisanship in all sporting contests
    And many a loud lament for our recent plight on the
    Tideway.)
      To you, then, all you languid and doré loafers
      On gilded college lawn and punt's sunny cushion,
      I commend that fellow there with bursting calves and
      forearms.
      A man of brightest mystery,
      Luke, if I could ever see

Behind your sweaty brow I'd be
Illuminatus for eternity.

Sweaty oarsman,
Snow-clouds above you,
Green water under your bottom,
  Could our eyes be strung together
  On the same thread,
  Ah, what a vision!
And ah, if only all my snarling friends
Could sit together at some golden table of the Lord—
A sweet, impossible symposium where:—
  Sybarite and coenobite
  Fast together at the feast;
  And herbivore and carnivore
  Devour the vegetable-beast.

  Introvert and extrovert
  Admire the inner-outer view,
  While egotist and altruist
  Adore the face of I-in-You.

But none were like my dead sons. And still their honied names,
Their loved names are murmured still in quads and summer
gardens.

"Her hair like the raven's glossy wing!" It was the ass,
The superannuated ninny of the Nineties,
Holding a pose of rapture, statuesque in Wadham.
Nay, sirrah . . . Yet, to be absolutely honest,
The idiotic words did flush my pride
And swell my chest to make the starch creak.
  And I can't honestly see that it's such a crime
  To feel a bit of pride in such a glorious
  Belle Dame de Trente Ans sans Merci.
Michael, debs' delight and violent hunting man,
Stared with mouth and eyes agape as I led her in
To the suddenly-silenced room of oafs and oloroso.

A LEARNED CITY

Ah, she's the brightest banner of the Lost Decade,
A sign and wicked symbol yet of all that wild
But withered alexandrian extravagance!
You know, chaps, we've missed a lot by being born
Ten years too late, and coming of age at last
In a dull age of economic obliquity.
Shall we resume, now, the wars of lily and turnip—
Alabaster youths setting their persian cats
On blazing Blues who fled howling from Trinity?
Or shall we march from the North with tiny, bony men,
Clench our yellow fists and raise to the morning light
Banners dipped in the martyred blood of Peterloo?

Had Hendrik lived to see his father's shamed and felled estate,
If only Nils had ducked his godly head from the winged
bullet—
Why then my two sons would have marched on the city side
by side;
My true sons would have driven the draped dons cackling
from college.
Ho, what a belly of black-bat gowns as the dons flee from their
dens!
And the wind shouts at last through all the crusty and besotted
caverns.

But now, ah Lucifer,
Bring me *light*
Before you fall again
And lurch me down to the dark.
  It does no good to
  Cry for the moon or
  Weep for little men
  With dusty mufflers and
  Abrasive cheek-bones.
  It does no good at all
  To visit certain sour streets

59

Where the women slouch and spit.
A woman shouted at me, and I
Was unmanned: I was unmanned.
An overgrown and sexless boy
With an artificial tongue, I
Was a prancing, derisory visitor
From a world of golden idiots.
No! By the light of *memory* I'll live.
My brother's hair again,
Frozen backwards from his temples:
Wings on the helmet of Hermes.
We lashed the freezing current of
The yelling Isar.
And the wind blew through us;
The sun pricked our pores;
The rain pierced our skin:
And girls—our eyes sucked them in:
Tiny models of girls
Played in the maze of my head.
   But now, in dreary February,
   Walking alone among the dead elm-trees,
   I quiver for you, my absent brother,
   Languid in white drill,
   Preparing a précis for His Excellency.
   I grieve for the motor-bikes:
   I weep for a Dick who never wished
   For the sweet sibilance of gossip,
   The whispered flattery of malice in
   Quad-corner; changing-room;
   The doorway of Hall above the clatter of knives and
   forks.
   (And one voice bellowed through
   The yapping of the Christ Church beagles.)

Or did they die with clear eyes turned to the evening sky?
Did they see in the red sky a golden world adying?
They knew that even the Sons of Glory dull and grow dim

When the world that lit them dies and all the days are grey as
dust.
   A golden brood, the boys of Nineteen Twelve, and rich
their relics:
A richer dust feathers a foreign soil, or works in the wold.
Nor even they could have lit the sun again by living on
In this our dead of day: not even Nils or dead de Bellay.

     Well then, Firkin Warlock, I would take you now
     To the junior common room for tea and plotting.
     I would feed your starved pretender's frame
     On oozing muffins, cratered crumpets;
     Anchovy toast and Gentleman's Relish.
       Royal Perkin, here's my loyal sword!
       (For we pretenders know that we
       Must hang together or hang separately.)

But after the news came of a death and a death, never a silent
House, but the woman's endless bibble-babble from dawn to
night.

     There's the bad angel—
     Loki? Lucifer?—
     He of the nether kingdom,
     He who often reeks from the gate
     Of a specially wicked college, and
     Is seen to shamble down the High
     Trailing a reek of gas and onions.
     And now by Mary, Hilda and Edmund,
     By Giles, John and Scholastica—
     By all the saints of Oxford, lo
     The sulphurous fellow stands hunched
     On the far bank, in a green blazer,
     Over the blessed waters of Isis.
       "Halloo, Arthur! You who were with me at the ferry,
       "Hell's aromatic bridegroom—what's with you
       "This day of thaw and the first breath of the damned
       "spring?"

A LEARNED CITY

When the college memorial was newly unveiled, and the gold
names gleamed,
Bliss, ever a sturdy pile against the "vulgar emotions",
Stood to con the names with thoughtful thumb on third chin,
And said, in mild and maundering tone:—"They were a
mixed lot."
  Such a prosaic *ass* you be, lying flat on the fallow
And never guessing that the same earth has grown a golden
crop.
Think you, sir, that each of these gold names is no more
Than a sign to summon a pinched or a spotty face, or a
braying voice?
Know you naught of war's quick and blazing alchemy?
Art blind, sir, to the late flowering of dead faces?
They are *not* as they were, nor any eye sees them so:
Ghosts or golden names—nothing of the young flesh now.
Phoenix-cornet-of-horse risen where once a flannelled fool
Lounged in the quad and swung an idle racket at the daisies.

  Mulberries had stained her bright yellow skirt:
  A silver sweat had flecked her deep-scooped temple:
  She sat without grace under the mulberry tree.
  But heavens, how she reigned and ruled in Worcester
garden,
  Sprawled and speckled there, in a circle of young
cavaliers,
  All dumbfounded by her silent sophistications.
    "Oh *mistress* mine!" Waddling water-birds:
    Sauterne on the tongue—a sweet recall of luncheon.
    And ah, the green eyes: I bask in a green light.
  Said I—or *may* have done: or *might* have done:—
  "Allow me, Jack, to introduce
  "My mistress of the month. And this, my dove,
  "Is Captain Abel, aide-de-camp
  "To Marshal Wittgenstein."
    Then, at the lake's edge,

Watching caddis grub, or sedge,
Reflected that in Styx or Lethe
No fish or fly could be.
How these sulphured rivers seethe!
How could a fish breathe?
And in England too
Many a sour factory brew
Fouls a living stream.
I saw the white bellies of bream
Pout on Horsea Mere
And rot in the meshes of the weir.

Bernard, my dear lad; viceroy of all the rich dead:
Bernard, who never changed among the faces fallen and
fouled.
None such live now as the four who rode along the Wall:
Our reading-riding party; powdered heather under hoof.
Mike de Bellay: Mullen, Paul and grave Bernard Carew:
M. C. J. de Bellay; gold leaf in rosy granite.
Aye Mike, and ever hewn, too, in "the Prof's" mind:
A reared cock and red comb. Scotland reared behind you.

Lady be good to me, as I shall ever be
Charming to *you*, no matter how you drone and buzz,
Talking of Ovid's metamorphosis
Into a sulphurous quack of love
In Languedoc and Aquitaine.
Be my Eve in the fatal orchards of experience:
Pluck for me now, my dove, thousands of those apples.

Listen, clown! Mike de Bellay had the girth of a great ox:
His cresting red hair rose in billows of bright joy.
His piping laughter pealed and shook along the border hills:
It bounded back to us from the famished fells of a dry summer.
And Mullen was the silver prince of a later age—say
Charlemagne's:

His court had learned courtesy, but remembered their
broadswords.
A young blade like a thrown knife that sings in an oak door:
He hummed and quivered as he walked in the wind of the
high fells.
And last of the dead I summon Paul, our green boy; our
silence:
Riding there he held us all in a bell of green silence.
Yes, even when Mike roared and Mullen hummed to the wind
Paul, whose eyes were filled with the green spring of next year,
Blew his silence into our heads and made our hearts still:
Mike's red roar died away in a green shade.

    Ha, they were men indeed in their dignity,
    Having the great advantage, don't you see,
    Of dying into immutability.
    Changeless Mullen; Uncle Hendy,
    Turned to marble statues by
    A gaffer's petrifying memory.
      But what did they ever know
      Of Professor Blumenthal on Boar's Hill?
      He smelt of stone and blood
      In that old fragrance of books and rosemary.
      He peered through thick spectacles,
      Wore ridiculous, green plus-fours
      And spoke with gluttony of his oppression.
      He held up on the tennis-court
      A green rubber hose
      In a dangling hand of broken knuckles.
      And he laughed as he meatily recalled
      The thud of rubber in a dark cell.

And I'd have sailed with Balder, too, when the war broke his
silence:
Thrice I begged for a soldier's coat, and thrice they said me
nay.

And Balder sailed away with all his godly companions:
But none could save Paul—none of his old feres of Asgard.
His blind brother brought him low—Hodur of the green Rhine:
And all his grey foes over the mud, they wept for Balder.
And no such stars were ever heard again in the May sky,
But drooping moons and suns that squealed and lurched across the sky.

That old buffoon
The yellow moon!
But when I reach your pocked and dusty face
I'll hang a magic lantern on your chin
And give you back your lost, classical grace.

"Kine die; kinsfolk die: self dies the same."
(Aye, but too late, outliving the last of the spring gods.)
"One thing I know that dies not ever—names of the noble dead."
(But when the world ends all names are naught again.)

And yet I saw
Nielson mount the hill of the wild boar,
And all the fleece of his hair
Blazed in a gold fire.

If Hermod, Balder's living brother had rode to Hel for him,
The fire of spring had come again to the wept-out waste of Asgard.
But Christian had rather make the world laugh; a dry laughter:
A thin rattle; parched hyenas dying in bone-dust.

I saw him, once, climbing the long hill of his garden
And the autumn sun was rising over the hazel-wood,

E   65

And all his rough white mane was set on fire.
I, at the bedroom window, saw him suddenly
Changed from the rank and sweating ape of the garden
gym
Into a Moses still glowing from Sinai.

And died the death, all my young souls. Damn their souls!
Damn, damn their selfish souls, they took themselves away.
The crystal waters of Oxford all befouled. Adultery!
The wicked witch has stirred a stew of foul adultery.

"Ho Archibald! Fisher of Men, ahoy!"
Punting by, and the long punt that scuds before him
Is innocent of any coiled girl, of course.
   Consider him now, the dank and holy Archibald
   Who sucked for my soul at school, and see how a dry age
   Has drawn his sickly vapours out of the damp flesh.
   A man, today, of singular authority,
   Dry as sandalwood, and in his disputations
   Witty and aromatic as a young Dominican.
   Is'nt it just *like* the rare fellow to punt alone
   On water silvered by a bright March wind,
   And empty, still, of any girls or gramophones.
Shall I this year, too,
Sweat on the cushions of punts,
Smelling the golden glue
As I hotly kiss
Pale Mrs Carew?
Shall I this year too,
Moored in the willow's tent,
Read *Le Roman de la Rose*
Aloud to you?

The moon has filled the quad again, like a tank of silver water:
Here was my silver keep. Here, at this hour, I read and reigned.
Sunk in saga was Nielson king of his own country:

Of all the eddas I, Nielson, have been lord and master.
Did I not wed the wild shore to these stained stones?
Gunnar's Sam was whelped again to hunt across the hill.
    Ah my feres of long ago, I've seen a sweaty Sigurd
    Mount the wide, worn steps to Hall, and drink deep
    Of gold and silver goblets in the Old Buttery.
    And many a brackish Loki lurks in All Souls and Balliol.

        Archibald enters the Cherwell as one who glides through
        Heaven's Gate.
        And really, I find it hard to credit such an amazing
        dehydration,
        Effected, after all, by just this river-rounded,
        Weed-and-watery city, rinced by the wet bells.
        Yet Archibald is now unpolished oak and elm;
        A scent of old stone, and only the fading breath
        Of holy incense on the dry, church air.
        A sacrament of work in his own person,
        Wirily bent to hoe his chalky garden soil,
        Or standing straight to read Augustine on a lectern.
        Opposing usury with dry, emphatic palms
        His plain argument, like a gregorian chant,
        Reproves the opalescent subtleties *we* blow.
        I see, when I listen to this much-altered Archibald,
        A spare land of holy but very clean peasants,
        In the manner, perhaps, of Grampa's flemish altar-piece
            Cedar-scented agrarian,
            Sedate anarchist of Christ,
            Ora pro Nobis.

He who can call the past and bring the dead to new life,
He marries age to age, and ever will be Time's master.
At this my desk no scholar-spider spun a grey web
Of dusty words to mend a laundry-list of Cretan Minos.
Live again, Thorgursson! From base and broken text
I brought a *living* Gunnar forth, and made Njal whole.

But why does Grampa talk of adultery;
Always mouthing the word "adultery",
And looks at me as if he thought
He thought he thought he saw, in the dim of the quad . . .
  Oh, to hell with all that!
  God knows I'm not perfect;
  A bloody fool at times;
  Egotistical as all
  The young are egotistical;
  Diffuse in my emotions;
  Intellectually extravagant;
  Lacking Faith and Charity,
  After the manner of the young.
  (But much attached to Hope,
  That *ballooning* virtue!)
And better the delicate vices of the young
Than to be deaf to all the shouted wrong
Done to a daughter and a ruined son.
Better even *my* swinishness
Than an old self-tortured egotist
Who never heard, above the yelps of his affronted
dignity,
Rubber hoses bursting the balls
Of certain *geehrte Kollegen*, those
Less fortunate professors over there.
Soon, soon I shall . . .
  He smells of red carbolic soap, and often makes
  A brutalised ablution of the delicate world.
  I hate his clean and cauterising red eye.

I believe that when Gunnar died no frown furrowed his face:
No grin gashed his face; he died unsmiling.
Thus *my* Gunnar dies. Thus have I lit a light,
A new light to wink and gleam from the sleeping page of the past.

  And yet it seems that Grampa's *Njal* appalled
  Meticulous scholars by the way he'd mauled

The true text, and horribly empurpled
That plain tale, until *all* was garbled.

A light suddenly shone on the page after four and forty readings:
Lo, after forty years, a crazy phrase slipped into sense.
Who knows that click in the head, the light shone on the dark:
The crooked made straight; the tight knot untied in the head.
   (And Olrik made a fool of: I saw his damned fool's face:
   I leaned back and closed my eyes and laughed at the Ass of
   Oslo.)

    And why should I
    Deny
    That often I
    Do indeed envy
    The sweet authority
    Of Archy's stone-grey eye?
       Well, I mean I . . . Mr Abel, sure
       I never meant that I would ever fall
       Into the pit of Christ where censers clang
       And puff their spicey clouds against the stink.
    And yet I do, I do still watch
    Out of the corners of both eyes,
    For any wisp of God in the wild skies.
    Oh for a revelation to ignite
    A burning Dick, a pentecostal youth,
    A fifty-tongued and holy Abberville!

The Oslo Ass, my everlasting spur and back-biter:
At first a mere mouse-squeak—a new dating of the Helgi Lays.
But soon a blunderbuss; mad charges; tack and nail
Bursting my door and splintered sunlight coming in like spears.
Sons dead! Wife gabbled to a quinsy! Dry rot!

And that great girl—Gulveig—roared and roared in the
azaleas . . .

    What! The daughter
    And my mother!
    Does he *dare*
    To speak of her?
      Drove her at eighty down the bypass:
      How she squealed with girlish joy.
      And after she'd gone did Simon say,
      "But your mother is an *angel*!"
    Oh mighty and angelic mother!
    Oh speeding Artemis!
    Oh you who enchanted all the young lords!
    Did I see
    All that Gulveig might have been
    But for that coarse, unloving sea-elephant,
    Her intolerable father?

Verily Ragnarok! The moon engulfed by the gulping wolf:
Papers and articles fly burning from Norway. Quick! Stamp
on 'em!
Or all this college room's afire, and books blaze on the shelves:
My blue translations burn, and Nielson's name shall be no
more
Than ash on the wind in Bergthorsknoll: ash across the sea.
    Oh adultery! Adultery! Adultery!
    A fouled nest. The lame eagle's nest is hen-befouled.

    Where once a mullion window peered at the front quad
    Is now an open-eyed sash window.
    But from that ghost of a mullion window
    Leans with wild eye and fist
    The Calvin of old Oxenford.
      Ora pro Nobis.

A LEARNED CITY

But turn, oh Prof, from that dark burner over the sea
To where an old and half-seen farmer hovers across a text.
An ancient face aglow, but gashed and garbled on the page
Until an O is made an A, and the full face shines.

Ah, the time will come when . . .
Tempus fugit, like a train.
But now I'll dwell on the small delights of the world—
A jaw-cracking yawn;
A sneeze in the high sun;
A rosy bath after football;
The pure seawater of an oyster;
A wall-demolishing pee after
Long dilation of the bladder.

Twice buried in new paint, the furrowed face of Sigurd:
First by the Old High German of romantic Niebelungs;
A second time by that velvet-capped and impudent harmonist
Whose swooning "Siegfried" clanks and roars from a tin
breastplate.
And I, like any restorer of Old Masters, scoured away
The gaudy paints, to show again the furrowed farmer's face.
But ever, over the North Sea, the grinning beast of Oslo
Faulted all my works. You be damned to devil and hell,
Olric, skulking in the Old Town . . . you be damned, oh . . .

Oh, oh,
March morning!
How my dough is risen!
How I tingle!
I can smell God
In the gas that bubbles
Out of Cherwell mud;
In a wind that puffs
Over Christ Church meadows,

Moist with cows
And soft with the worn stone,
The crumbled bread
Of Corpus Christi.
  Last spring
  You and I,
  Oh Wolf, the Second Secretary,
  Sniffed the wind above
  The summer palace of
  Our wigged and sworded fathers.
  Sordid fathers!

Abel patters—no, he *titters* by on pointed toes:
The evil elf has darkened the whole quad as he billows by.
  I know what such as Abel says: "An old bardic fraud!"
  They call me a false spinner of mist-bedrunken mumbo-
jumbo.

  Nay, Sir Orpheus,
  Richard Hero,
  Never look over your shoulder
  At a spring that's sprung and gone.
    Running skyward up
    The cracked willow trunk,
    As if God the Dove
    Had chosen me alone
    To save from the dragging grave.
    Now I . . . jump the . . . green railings,
    Land where the rivers meet
    And lean lightly back
    From the hatching waters of,
    Hithering-thithering waters of
    The Lady Isis, Queen of Egypt.

But what do they know of an old text ten years tortured:
What do they know of a blurred page most purely pried!

Aiy! Aiy! I see the hosts of Midian mandering near:
Bliss and Abel—faugh! Hodgett, Wade and Prout the
Lamb!

I remember that day of blazing buffoonery,
Perkin in Christ Church garden, where the red-hot pokers
Drove me to wilder and wilder revelries of talk.
Debauches of the mind! I love to lie in the sun
With golden lads around me whose immortal laughter
Bubbles in my head like an old wine of Samos.
    Hey there, Poacher! No such classical pretensions,
    please!
    You never yet sailed among the Cyclades
    Nor heard the sirens sing across sicilian seas.
    The tone was induced, I dare say, by a simple longing
    To be rid, for a while, of this romantic berserker
    And to walk again between Venus and Hercules.
    And I think of another old man whose easy belly
    Moves before him like a genial bow-wave
    Over the mown and breathing lawns of Ramillies.
    "Books in the portico!" His sunny, southern love
    For Pliny's learned villa; toga'd figures strolling
    Side by side between the balmy cypress trees.
Or think of him: and him: and him! I think of twelve
Incredibly bright harbingers of Abberville.
I mean, in a single life, to be all, to be *all* of these.

And now are all the young men but frail and frantic Gynts;
But useless buttons on the brocaded waistcoat of the world.

    Regarding me, regarding me,
    As if by peering he could just make out,
    Under the swarthy skin of Abberville,
    A mountain-troll entombed, but crying out.
      God, that I were a Matthew Miles,
      That perfection of a man,

Cricketer and pianist,
Scholar, poet, quiet walker,
Ambulant philosopher—
All that I could never be.

Liar, coward, mountebank; faithless fraud and boaster:
Aye, Peer was all of these, and worse than all the rogue
Was NOTHING at last but a husk of NOTHING. Nothing at all.
And so it is with any who feels the spike, the spike of it.

Oh you who begged me never to forget you,
Lying among old apples in the oast-house!
You who prayed to your inconceivable future face—
"Never disown me!
"No, never deny this boy when you supplant him!"
Know this, bucolic Dick, wherever you are,
That I, the young man scarfed and lordly,
Have neither turned against you nor denied you.
No, nor ever will be other than
The dungy boy who lay among the apples.
    But subterranean men with skin as grey as steel
    Shuffle down St Giles like the ghosts of Passchendaele.
    And I no more to them nor they to me
    Than ash on a grey sea.
Nor *he* to me, my dark, dead father;
Father's body curled and mildewed
On an old farm waggon.

"A King! A Kaiser!" Peer would be. Oh wretched pretenders;
The swart, southern faces of two miserable pretenders.

Piety? Piety?
(A furry mould on military gaiters.)
Pity? Was it pity I felt?
(Flakes of dry dung on the waggon-spokes.)

A LEARNED CITY

Horror? Horror of the dead?
(He lay in the farm-waggon, trundling up the hill
Like someone overlooked by history, following
A mile behind the cavalcade of the war-dead.)
    And I must run and run, away or after him,
    Around these looping bends of the Cherwell till . . .
    I see the heavy girls across the river,
    The ladies of St Hilda's playing tennis.
    And I see the spring tide of bicycles
    Belling and swirling over Magdalen Bridge.

She cried out in the azaleas that I had never loved her moody monsters,
Drackish louts. Eh, what a she-devil crying there!
But how can I love the brood of these blind and bitter years,
The spawn of a sallow age? I do abhor the yellow years.

    The good lady! Ah, the good lady!
    And she, in her clumsiness,
    The strawberry stain flushing cheek and neck,
    Deserves to be loved at last.
        For I was never Prince Orestes in
        The family *Kreise*, nor was ever she
        To the dead king a wayward Clytemnestra.
    I resolved it, I
    Made up my mind in
    The apple-loft to be
    Neether, neither
    Slayer of my father
    Nor of my mother.
    I would rather *not* be—
    Be a nothing, nowhere, in no
    Way at all than that
    Hidden Clubfoot of Thebes, or
    Of Argos that prig
    And wronger of wrongs.

Bernard, dear boy, limping through another Oxford spring,
You turn stone to brimstone and all the Turl to twisted lava.

    "Clive! Think of the devil! Do we dine tonight?"
    "Rose my love, a penny for *your* sweet thoughts."
      Pop-pop-popular Dick,
      Ain't you sick
      Of this fatuity,
      This honey-sweet popularity?
    But oh remember now your mother in
    The days of spring and folly by the river!
    She who trusted to your fortitude,
    Your serpent's cunning,
    To snatch the elder brother from the spicey claws,
    Of sphinx or dark Medusa in old Egypt.
      Wearing a pith helmet? Gripping his paw
      Under a date-palm in a shuddering oasis?
      Well I do know something of *gorgons*, do I not?!

But oh my Bernard, not with such a *burning* breath can we
Level the counting-house and fire filthy Leadenhall.
Else we'd burn all flat, burn it black as the soot of hell
And leave a hell fit only for the red trolls to dung and dance on.
Nay rather shall we climb, only the two of us,
High in the frozen sky above the money-sick cities.

    How he plagues us with his prophesy,
    Professor Nielson in the shrubbery!
    Oh thou sylvan god of the lecture-hall,
    Art *thou*, then, so bright and beautiful!
      Egg! A flake of yellow on his blue lapel,
      The yachting blue. And how many thousand eggs, old
      man,
      Have you, in sixty-five years, *manducated*?
      How many eggs, Nielson? Say five a week,
      And sixty-five by fifty-two is three thousand

Three hundred and eighty: multiply by five is . . .
Six-teen thousand nine hundred eggs,
Introduced by spoonfuls, trod by the white horses,
Over the pink hill dragged to the chiming tonsils.
Down they glugged and squeaked their alimentary passage
To meet digestive acids in the noisy stomach,
Melt and drown there, giving up the ghost.
And then the ghosts of eggs, in bubbles of marsh gas,
Rose where the swallowed eggs had dropped, and issued forth
To burp and belch from Nielson's unasham√©d lips.
Meanwhile the mess of melted yoke and soused albumen
Entered the mazy tubes of the great and small intestine,
To bulge and rumble there in ever-changing substance.
And now they sweat and strain into the back passage,
Burn in the blown-up rectum with a hot impatience
To prod and press the tender rearward of the sphincter.
Then are those same eggs layed again
To vilify a jakes, contaminate a privy
And send their hot reek to the sky for God's delight.

For once, on the Jotunheim, I did take fire from the eye of God:
All the fire of the high snows burned my body up.

Janet also scowls at the age; they *all* do,
All who've passed thirty and look bitterly back
At the long green vomit of their youth behind them.
    But oh my age, I prick my ears
    To hear your overtures.
    I stare incessantly round
    Every one of your horizons.
    And if tomorrow's sun should rise in the western ocean
    I shall dive *that* way from the coast of Kerry.

Ah twentieth century,
Glittering fourth decade of it,
And twenty-second year of Richard!
   Age of Complexity!
   We fall, by entropy,
   Into diversity.
Age of Hope!
A plane flew so high
That it left the sky
And is sailing now
In that breathless clime
Where space is eating time.
And snowmen fight the phoenix on the wind
That blows out of the Finite-Unconfined.
   Age of Drama!
   Spain's abusive plateau where
   Dynamiting miners crawl
   Under whining tanks that bite
   The ancient mould of the olive-groves.
And we hear that Professor Faustus looked dryly down
from a window in Balliol
And saw, though his eyes were dimmed by the smoke of
many wicked retorts,
A thousand homunculi, or dwarfs, tramping past the
college
And silently asserting that they would prefer BREAD to
new knowledge.

Then was I GOD's CHILD: I was the burning child of God,
And in my joy MAD. But when I came down again to the
valley . . .

Ah, my poor dove! My lady of a dead age
Sniffing the faded scent of the *Ars Amatoria*,
How can *you* breathe the new fires of the world?

78

An age of salamanders: I'm a salamander.
No dear, you are *not*, but one who always needs
A delicate adjustment of the temperature.
Her mute discomfort on the grass in Worcester Garden:
Her "wry" look; the martyr to her own
Rejection of the martyr's satisfactions.
"Divine!" she moans:
"Precious!" she groans,
Showing her age
By her sprightly-faded language.
   She was of that "set"
   Who danced the clay hard
   Over the war dead.

. . . I heard, again, the groaning of an age in the pangs of a
false labour,
And saw, at last, *mice* cast from the womb of the snow mountain.
All these men are mice or midgets. Sam, my dying dog,
Dies for that he stifled in the sour, milk-sodden air.

   Enough, enough in any case
   Of such *conservatory* loving.
   (Twining cucumbers that sweat in frames.)
      Incisive Ripper—ah, my Jack the Knife!
     "Everything is what it is
     "And not another thing."
   To which I tingle like
   An apple touched by the frost.
   "Everything is what it is
   "And not another thing."
   An acid singularity in place
   Of a blurred duplicity.
     (And oh, may *I* be what I am
     And not another thing!)

All things mixed and mingled now; all adulterate:
I . . . oh I shall welcome *any* death from such living.

Pete, my chum,
Fishtail roaring
Over Magdalen Bridge.
   Chums? Or are they only this year's audience;
   Enough eyes, enough ears, enough applause
   For the Golden Ass—Lucius or Bully Bottom—to feed
on?
   He suffers, here, a donkey metamorphosis
   And brays for the brazen laughter of his boon-imbibers.
Into *Mawdlin* then I came, gold-burning,
(Cousin of Calf, by the bewildered Jews adored)
Clopping past the portly porter's fish-regard.
Into the Mag-da-lene I came, with golden thong
Avast between my legs—an aureate tumescence
Plunged to the hilt in Mary's cave, the Master's Mistress.
   Then did Lucius Abberville quaintly experience
   Divergent emotions, motor impulses which drove
   This way the vestigial man—thither the Ass.
   As it were a pillar of fire within the dark cloisters,
   And this to the Ass was fearful: by GOD he would flee,
   An his hoofs would carry him, far as ISLIP upstream.
   (There did Adam the Ox fall among the cowslips.)
   But equally a sweet treble trembled from the chapel,
   Promising frank forgiveness for previous peccadilloes,
   And never more the lady lorn to haunt my stable.
   This drew, of course, the *man*, or what was left of him;
   And, seeking solace, obsolute absoletion,
   Broke he toe from hoof and footed featly forward.
   And came, with loud clattering step, into the cloisters,
   Dark as tomb or mausoleum, where the ports
   Admit no more than three shafts of gothic sunlight.
And was he better suited, Andrew Abberville,
To lie in such a shadowed bower of English stone,
Under the towery deck where ship-boys sing in the sky?
Were you better lain in old stone, Wolf,
Under the crennelation of Norman and Early English,
Under a Decorated shade, or Perpendicular?

A LEARNED CITY

Yes fellows—you who never knew my brother—
He was as English as the spire of Salisbury,
The nave of Gloucester or the worn steps at Wells.
Perfectly suited by his elegiac nature
To this untrodden square of martial piety
Where holy grass is warded by the battlements.
An *English* man, as many of his kind do, died
Among the hot bazaars and spiced tombs of Islam,
Far, far from the stone he breathed when he was a boy.

He was too lordly, that dear lad, for an age of the black trolls:
Born for a better age, how could he breathe your fumey air?
  I mind as if it were yesterday the lad's first voyage:
  Out of Svinafell we rode on a north wind to Orkney.
  And this Andrew Edvardson, a shaver of ten years,
  Hung at the stern and dipped his bright fingers in the wake.
  He raised a brined and bubbling face, crying:—"See,
  Grampa,
  "Here I belong with Hogni Helmsman. Let me stay here
  ever!"

  But though he was as English as this monkless cloister of
  old Magdalen,
  Yet there was something almost eastern in his alabaster
  profile.
  A young prince of Serbia or Dalmatia, say, where many
  streams
  Of the Mediterranean mingle, under the hot marble
  palaces
  Of Diocletian, that maligned and self-obliterating
  emperor.
  Or further east—something Graeco-Albanian, with a
  faint whiff
  Of Arab in the hewn, deserted face; cousin, of Shem's
  descent,

To Jules the Jew. (Remember that I dine with Jules on
Monday.)
    A gauzy figure through my grey mosquito-net, Sir
    Julian Manville
    Stood like an angel of annunciation in the white door-
    way
    And broke the news and broke the dream with
    crumbling lips and dry tongue.
    And I, seeking Isis, move through the summer haze of
    the River Isis—
    Away from all that maze of muddy channels in the
    Delta where
    My brother Osiris lies in shreds, and melts into the
    Nile mud.
I mean . . . I mean . . . not there. But my eyes are still
crusted with salt.
My eyes are salted still. How can I see
The dwarfs' far faces, or the hand
Of a mangled and garrulous Herr Professor?

Ventured then, I and my feres, southward to the sun's
Parched and rotting island. 'Twixt the giant pillars wheeled
Into a tideless sea, and the sail's shadow on the sea before us.
We of the yellow hair shall burn the festered seas of the South.

    But *you* I see only too easily in your hot, blue parlour,
    My weekly instructress in the courtesies of *Frauendienst*.
    Janet sighed and said that I surely didn't expect *happiness*
    From any form of love's service. I was to train my grief,
    My wailing for my brother's death, into the stately
    motions
    Of an antique pain, to ape *in saeculo*
    The cold dance of the stars;
    The convolutions of the stellar angels.
      I can't bear it any longer:
      No, I can't bear

That foul-weather friend who feeds,
Like a damned hen-vulture,
Only on the carrion of unhappiness.
But now I'm out of that dark, stone tunnel:
I've reached the sun's arcade and the fallow-deer,
And must, for my manhood, force apart
Eyelids crusted with salt.

Sicilia on the port! And here we'll sink our anchor deep
And rule the soft adulterate race of Greek and Saracen.
I, exiled to the lazy lands, shall breed a race
Of golden giants where the Romans rotted in their armour.

How cold a vacancy the world has suffered,
The ignorant world which scarcely notices
This hole the shape of Andrew Abberville.
   But through it an icy wind begins to blow:
   Ice chokes me, filling my mouth and throat,
   Coating my lungs with ice.
   What a sudden darkness in the open sun!
   What a monstrous old snowman against the sun!
   I come to an unwilling stop in the presence of my
   grandfather's premature ghost,
   He an accuser,
   His age accusing my youth
   Of horrible offences,
   Unbelievable offences.

But once again, damn it, once again I must heave back
To a vile age. (Oh farewell, my feres of the bright seas!)
A heavy task. Aye, the two so snakily entangled
On Gaudy Night, in a cranny-corner of the Front Quad.
Bernard betrayed. His bitch with drooped dugs clutched by
the four legs
Of that orang-utan, my daughter's monstrous misbirth.

Stink of snakes! I'll bring the brute to book: I'll show him his
face
In the true mirror of my eye; and he shall fall in a faint to see it,
Fall down in a faint—oh, he shall be turned to stone, nor ever
Rise again to writhe with the witch in a wet bed.

> I wonder if his hanging face
> Hangs so heavily because
> Of what he saw with his own eyes,
> On Gaudy Night, under the rose.

With these eyes I saw, and I standing in the window there,
Filthy rumour taking flesh. How my eyes were sickened!
"Lies! Lies!" I used to shout the snickering rumour down:
I trod it down as a gaitered keeper stamps the hissing snake.

> Through a crystal web of hair,
> Threads lit by a pale star,
> I saw Grampa's forehead lour
> Like the nursery blackamoor.
> And, burning by my darling's ear,
> The rose flamed in velvet fire.

But under the black wall-roses I saw them twined together:
Black of mien was he, but his barrel cased in white starch.
Those gorilla arms clutched to the white, creaking chest
The snake-lady. Snake and monkey coupling under the rose.

> Though his eyes were hidden in
> The black disk of his face upon
> The yellow window, yet my own
> Eyes shrivelled under that inspection.

My eyes were turned sour by the buckling of the two-backed
beast:

I hid my eyes: I shut the lids over the soured jellies.
Crack your cheeks! Stuck together by spit, sweat and seed:
Gealed together at mouth and breast, at belly, fork and thigh.

> Oh hidden and fiery eye,
> Burning, burning in that elderly
> Black, enframed head of a dirty
> Old man, Susannah's spy,
> How did you ever dare to say
> That it's *I* am uncleanly?

Burning! Burning! I saw them twisted together against the
wall:
I would burn all lechers. I would fuse them, truly.
    And yet 'tis known for a riggish world; 'tis well known
    For foul corner-couplings. Gods and gilded flies go to't.
    Art amazed, then, by the Lady Janet's lecheries?
    Stand'st in amaze, old Prof, at grandson's gross and ruttish
capers?

> Aye, but here's the last laugh,
> Basiliskine peeping Prof!
> 'Twas'nt that aging waif
> In my arms, but my future *wife*.
>   Oh presence of all my future life
>   Through all the seasons of my grief,
>   Under old castles of the faith,
>   In rivers bubbling with new birth,
>   Wherever the wind blows from the grave.

And maybe *he* felt the grave-wind on his empty leg:
How did hornéd *Bernard* feel when he heard about his wife?
That she was a lewd bitch? Eh, our roaring pack-leader?
Eh Frenchy? Darky? Eh, you bedamnéd, dirty dog?

A LEARNED CITY

What is he *talking* about?
What?
The damned importunate
Old goat!

A damned impertinent ... A damned ... Bernard, set upon
him!
Sir Bernard, with your wooden leg ye'll hulk the lecher down.

    Opening eye of a new day,
    Flower of Lethe's bank, and joy
    Of our forgetting, ah how kindly
    You can clear the trammelled eye!

For sure he'd have his eye wiped of *that* grit upon it!
Aye, an he could he'd wipe away the horned hobbler.

    As if *I* could ever pain
    Fired brick or pumice-stone,
    Or that pickled soldier-man
    Salted in a bloody brine!

Salted in bitterness; fired by the flames of his own anger:
Aye, sir, he's fired by now to fire the whole world.

    He was of my father's race,
    Stupefied by bitterness,
    Bitter as an old curse
    Muttered in the dust of Argos.

For old curses, eh, they do so *magicate* a man:
They do so *mythify* a cuckold out of all feeling.
And so, for the lout, this man was fired to brick in ancient wars
And feels *naught* of pain, for sure, though he be unmanned.

A LEARNED CITY

Well, and what of *Christian*?
Is *he* a feeling man?
Can he feel the ancient pain
Of a fatherly damnation?

Carew came to his bloody loss among the damned of Pilkem:
His leg dropped and drowned in the rich mud of Langemark.
And where *then* was our gloried god of the football field?
Awash in wet sheets: pewling and bubbling in a bib and tucker.

And where was the Lady *Gulveig* then?
Where was your daughter, old man?
That great, grieving woman
Was going mad for a father's affection.

I grieve at Bernard's grief and gall. I do bemoan his anger:
And yet, God's teeth, I do most mournfully understand it.
To lose a leg in the botched wars for an old bitch of a land,—
He found naught to fret him there, but limped right manfully.
But to lose wife and manhood then, to an unweaned lout!
Aye, that was a dark sun would scorch any man.
And so the easy boy Carew, Henrik's hailfellow,
Was plague-stricken last year and burns with the red fever.

And what of *Magersfontein*,
Eh, my old soldier-man?
Did the foe squeal and run
From fierce, fire-breathing Nielson?

Love cools: friendship falls off: lies do abound:
Oh, I would breathe a melting fire on this befallen world.

Damn them, damn them all—
This loveless and god-awful
Prof in corsets, crammed full
With memories of the most terrible

Battles he never fought in, till
The whole
Man's a most contemptible
Backward-twisted denial
Of all that's hopeful,
All that's honourable.
 And then this burnt accuser swaying down the steps
 from hall—
 I find his gnarled and twisted stick utterly awful.
 He believes in ever-bountiful
 Fountains of virtue in the poor and pitiful,
  Yet is worse than parched within: he's all
  Charred and powdered like a used spill.
And then this serpent lady moaning her stale
Particulars of courtly love and adultery. What drivel!
Brr! The snakey wetness of her legs, the coil
Of cold arms around me till
Nearly the whole
Of my life was squeezed out of my broken shell.
And now she adds tears to the total
Of her lascivious injuries, the old she-devil!
 I say DAMN THEM ALL TO HELL!
But oh my eye of the new day, my DAISY
Of the green and gasping water, and the dizzy
Spring spawning in the hatchery!
We shall never look back, Daisy,
Nor ever be changed by Janet's witchery
To pillars of salt that sparkle dryly
Like those old ones, those who petrify
In crystal rage under a dead sky.

Keep me in temper! I will not be mad, not mad against
The horrid spring and the young men of the spring stretching
their arms.
You sir! Sir Green Oaf! Sir Bully Bottom awaking!
Be damned yet for what you left behind you in the spring.

There's my river apparition,
Rising in my last June
As a sedge or olive dun
Spins its churring wings upon
The rolling skin of Eden.
   Oh God of the River
   Who brought our boats together,
   Stem against stern above the weir!
   Like a rosy nenuphar
   You budded on the green water,
   And I grinning above you in the hot air,
   A clown; a steamy satyr.
And now come fly with me, my bird,
Far, far from the dead
Stones and groves and atrophied
Dons and dames of this Dunciad.

You! *You*! Ever-denying spirit; damnéd Abel!
All the old stones of the city crack under his eye.
They, too, would burn all down; those shouters
And bearded rotters who march against our tumbling citadel.
He first, the spy who questions every tower and stone:
Then the horded levellers and shouting mutineers.

   For I have heard the summer cry
   Of hope from that burning country
   Where a dusty misery
   Flowers in the almond tree.
      And in the embattled olive grove
      We shall try our northern love
      As the white-toothed peasants prove
      That the yeast of love may give
      Lightness even in the grave.

'Tis worse work, I hear, to dig graves i' the frozen tundras:
A million graves, I hear, for those who once wagged the beard.

Those who bore the bomb and wagged their beards at the mob
Have cooled their younger heat, I hear, in those ice-boxes.

> Look how the dappled fallow-deer
> Snuffle the wet stony air
> Of Magdalen melting by the river.
>> Oh we must fly together far
>> From clerk and wry philosopher,
>> From the parched prof and the Bas Bleu
>> Under the magnolia.

Aye, now the young eagle would soar *above* his late crime:
Now he outsoars the lamed cuckold and the bereft witch.
'Tis love of a lass, and surely a sweet love that soars him far
From the learned city where his late "love" lies acursing,
And the wounded husband, now diswifed as once he was
unlegged,
Lights the torch of himself to set the dry world afire.

> And am *I*, then, the youth carbuncular,
> An oaf in his arrogance, with the power
> To emasculate a gunner officer
> And leave *a woman* shaking on the floor?
>> Such a power . . .
>> A new power . . .
>> An acquisition of new power among the invulnerable
>> elders, and by means of it I take my place in the pain-
>> ful, elaborate and fateful manœuvres of the grown-ups.
>> Alarming, is it?
>> Shameful?
>> An insufferable vision of the wounded couple to whom
>> I behaved with such . . .
>> But also intoxicating, intoxicating!

The scoundrel! Oh, a most damnable and hard-hearted rap-
scallion!
A curse be on him now. All my curses on his head.

A most damnable old reactionary!
   Hell, being the oldest pit, he tries to dig it again
   And people this Sheol with all honest and rebellious
   men.
   But it's *he* that stinks of the pit: we belong to the sun,
   To the first light in the sky, rosy and apple-green,
   And to every flaming horizon.
Oh Spain, Spain!
What is it that breaks the crust of sullen plain
And ancient, bare-backed mountain?
Come Daisy, my love, let's eat the morning, and ourselves
be eaten,
For this hell-bound antiquary is much better forgotten.

Much is better forgotten for your peace. But look! I show
A certain stump of fevered flesh, strapped to yellow oakwood.
The skin is gathered together like a suet-pudding skin:
The bright scars, the raised weals of six centipedes.
And yet the prodding stump of bone may still be felt there:
A rounded ending, filed to smoothness by an army sawbones.

   What a pudding of pain!
   Will it, will it split and
   Burst forth a froth of bloody dough
   With a squeal?
     How shall I sleep tonight?
   For hark
   To the squeal of pain; or is it, is it
   The ancient hatred whinnied from the spinney?
     Now then you-all,
     Dearly-beloved,
     Sweet companions of my younger days,
     Why do you stand so still in the cold wood,
     And why are all your leathern backs squared against
     me?
     Matt! Matthew! *You*, Matthew Miles!

91

(Where the green witch thins to the music of snakes
  And the well in the wood falls to eternity.)
And you're of the band, too, Abel, pronouncing:—
"Whereof one may not speak
"Thereof one must be silent."
Meaning *me*!
And Friar Archibald, forsooth!
Holy Archibald is there,
Mouthing a virtuous christian curse upon me.
Auch Simon and all
The gold-braying nobs of Peckwater Quad
Have taken to abuse me with their nostrils.
Also bony Sam the Cowboy
Stands like a black statue of Lincoln under the trees
And virtue is reared against me everywhere
And I am become as wicked as Simon Legree.
        But ah, thank you! Hearty thanks to you, sir! But it's
        Only the Bad Angel, holding out a sticky palm to me.
        The demon cries, his palm wet and his hot eye firing
        upon
        A stump of tortured red flesh.
        "You shall be ever a rank hyena
        "Ever of the lowest order, and
        "Barbarous with rancid-buttered locks."
And spring? The spring?
An idiot laugh:
Feet on the stairs:
Feet mounting the stairs:
Feet about to kick my oak down:
Feet to kick me through the window.
In spring my enemies curse from the stairheads.
Spring, spring, season of suicides!

O my dead sons of long ago who died to make their father a
fool;
Curse ye the Lord who miscreated you, or be ye cursèd by the
empty sky!

A LEARNED CITY

O my yet-living son, thou pale and drunken ghost who haunts
the cloisters and the butteries;
Curse ye the Lord for miscreating you, or be ye curséd by the
empty sky!

> She said, bidding adieu; "*Au fond,* my dear,
> "What are you but a frivolous vulgarian!"
>> And you Andrew, limping brother,
>> Rising from a corner of the ante-room,
>> Why do you turn away from dreaming Dick
>> A face as smooth as ivory or polished bone?

O Abel, twisted devil of a man and everlasting Jew, thou who
scurries to All Souls by night and weaves a plot to darken all
our lights; Curse ye the Lord who miscreated you, or be ye
curséd by the empty sky!

> And that south-eastward voyage for which I longed—
> Mandarins of wisdom:
> Dulcimers and dusky maids;
> A humming peace, I dreamed, in the shade of a banyan
> tree—
> Now I'm checked, I'm halted, yes I am detained
> By the glaring odours of the hot canal; I . . .
> Egypt! Land of the Book of the Dead wherein I watch
> The tomb of a boy-king, and oh, oh,
> The sudden self-murder of . . .
> Proconsular and cool as evening, how he did scorn me.
> How he scorns me still, I well know, for this gross persist-
> ence in outliving him; this grossness of the living flesh and
> all the greedy senses of a great body.
> And in Egypt I can also hear the scarlet trumpet of con-
> volvulus which blow across the rich tombs of pharoahs
> and governor-generals. For the dead, in that country, are
> the most damnable boasters, knowing that all the spices

of a rich land can never hide the pulsing stench of their
fragmentary bones and liquefying organs.
Oh filed bone! Oh stump of suet!

O my dead and unknown grandson, you who died early;
Curse ye the Lord for miscreating you, or be ye curséd by the
empty sky!
O Bliss, soft-spoken sodomite who takes his holidays with
young men in Venice and murmurs latin verses in a breath
of port; Curse ye the Lord who miscreated you, or be ye
curséd by the empty sky!
Bliss, blesser of old wines and spirits, carver of ugly quips and
cruel wittings; editor of Martial; beast, a beast!
Curse ye the Lord who made a beast of you, or be ye curséd
by the empty sky!

    And I, Perkin, shall to the gallows.
    I'm to be hanged for my pretensions.
    The king, the king, his heart a wrinkled walnut,
    His face—look and see!—Father's face.
    Nay, he will not see me: he won't hear me.
    And so for a mere prank, a jape, my neck shall feel
    The burning rope, the hairs that tickle my soft skin, and
    then . . .
    Eyes . . . neck . . . Father! Father!
    Father in Heaven!
    Timor Mortis Conturbat Me.
    How shall I sleep tonight?

O Beastly Bliss who sighs for his rotten house in the South, his
villa of Malcontenta where horrible things are done by day
and night and a green slime, they say, is creeping up the
painted walls;
Curse ye the Lord who made a beast of you, or be ye curséd by
the empty sky!

A LEARNED CITY

O All Souls, where the soul of each proud fellow wallows in
sloth, billows with greed for the next Feast;
Curse ye the Lord for walling up so many bitter heads in that
prison!
And O Balliol, where ugly scotsmen brew a wormy froth of
Bannion-brau and plot to undo my Tommy Wood, my right-
ful heir;
By ye curséd by the empty sky!

He went stumping across a dark bridge, across
A river greened by the familiar vices of this city.
And there, where Carew stumps, sprawls the stumped
Body of a policeman, dripping his blood into the Seine.
Under the windy taffrail of a bridge . . .
Step no further! Clump no nearer me!
Major of the *Polizei*, corrector of . . .
   No, nor you neither, Lady of the Snakes,
   Mailed madame, scaled signora, weeping
   Cold tears; poison tears,
   Writhe no nearer me, or I shall . . .
   Mercy upon me, Lord, for the terror of death possesses
   me.

O my clumsy daughter—what a fool!—screaming in the
bushes that I'd never loved the black foreigners you bore;
Be thou curséd for the fool's faith you follow.
O Eddy Welburn, dead at last and never Earl of Bulmer, little
crazy squire of my moon-bewildered daughter, O thou who
never spoke me a word back through all that winter evening
in the palace;
Curse ye the Lord who made a proud boor of you, or be ye
curséd by the empty sky!

Young men, the well-formed in body, but
In mind simple, in will bullish and blind,

In you I looked for some bright mystery of God's blessing
Wherein I, too, would float to a heavenly illumination.
But they too, my one-time friends in the arc-light of fame,
Stand in the cold greenwood, leather-backed,
Where snake and fungus fill the air with poison.

    And what's *he*, this cringing Abberville,
    But a man already bloated with identity,
    A demi-English youth, and
    Born in the month of Sarajevo,
    Spotty, gross and—longing to please everyone—ob-
    sequious.

Oh I must slink away from this merciless arena!
Oh I feel the eyes of a hundred contemptuous men staring
down at my blemished face from all the tall windows of
this college!
Oh to be hidden forever from the eyes and tongues of men
and women!
How shall I sleep?

Oxford, Oxford, city of rivers fouled and wisdom lost, all your
pates are emptied now of aught but gossip that gustles like
dead leaves; the suck and snort of gluttony; the honey-flood of
flattery; plots by dirty paws entwined; and lust, a bellow rising
from the dark corners of quadrangles and old walled gardens!
Curse ye the Lord for miscreating you, or be ye curséd by the
empty sky.

    No no, not in Lethe nor in Styx either
    Could a fish breathe or a rising nymph
    Come up living to the surface of the poisoned water.

      And now the living streams of England are all polluted,
      Black with slag, rainbow-flecked with petrol and
      crude-oil.
      Deadly soaps have foamed and scoured the living
      water:

Gases bubble from the submerged pipes of factories
And all the clear rivers are stained to the poison blue of
copper-sulphate.
I saw the white bellies of a million dead fish—
Trout and salmon; chub and dace; roach and perch;
Bream, barbel and pike; eels as straight as pokers—
I saw them block the weirs and rot at the lock-gates.
And the stink rose from the valleys and rolled across
the hills,
And all England stank of sour chemicals and rotting
fish.
How shall I sleep again?
How shall I dare to stand on Magdalen Bridge again and
gaze down at the dead boys drifting below me on the slats
of rotting punts and disabled motor-boats?

O Albion, melting away; a mooning Empire!
Even the scotch pines, those trees that fight the wind with blue
fists, are dropping down their own trunks in rolls of melted
resin.
I saw the Isle of Mull turn to treacle.
And the men in white drill are sprawled in cool verandas now,
glugging their iced grog and fouling the fanned air with boasts
of their adulteries.
The while midgets thrive and seethe at home, a cloud of
whining midges in the mart.
And here the towers of the university are stuffed with a hairy
sloth of great white worms, reared up in each tower and
bulging—grey bladders of worm-flesh—through all the em-
brasures, oriels and casements.
Foul! Foul! And this my hand that touched it must be wiped
and wiped, for it smells of mortality.
I will scald this hand, and then . . .
Blow up the island . . .
See the adulterous morsels of the land splash, soggle and sink
in the eastern and western seas.

G　　　　　　　　　　97

"Uncle Christian!" (Oh my God!)
Oh you translucent prawn of a man!
Let me by, for God's sake, and you be nothing more
Than a breath, on the summer air, of stale whisky.
 But "Well done!" he breathes like a husk of barleycorn.
 "Congrats, congrats on doing down
 "That lady-pythoness and that grim
 "Stumping fire-dog, my brothers' long-lingering crony.
 "Good for you, best of nephews, make them squeal . . ."
A ghost! He should have died ten years ago.
He tries to breathe me into his company.
Jump away! Oh jump beyond him now and run
Away, away from the ruined uncle and all this peeled
exposure to the eyes of beastly despising men.
Run, run into the cool shade of these arches.
Libera Nos a Malo!
 Clever, clever Jack Abel
 Would not smile, sitting aloof at high table.
 And when I sconced you, Simon, at dinner
 You would not raise your tankard to a sinner.
 Holy Archibald,
 By my green sins you are appalled.
 Sam in the Turl, Sam of Idaho,
 Turned away a face of bony sorrow.
 Luke, oarsman of Isis,
 Rowed sternly by me. Why, why is this?
 Why do my friends cut me! Why,
 If all of them cut me dead I must surely die.
 And in my sweet youth I!
Fecal magician! You, de Graillon! Under your neat grey
cloth
Stale shit crumbles. *I* know!
Nor did you ever cure, kneeling to an empty throne,
The slow putrescence of the arse-hole.
 So is it, too, with Spanish cardinals who seem to smell
 Of swooning church-lilies, myrrh and incense,
 But who, if you sniff harder, cannot help sweating

The sharp acidulous smell of those busy worms
Which toil in the crutches of old men.
And crumpled kings slobber in dusty gold palaces:
Archdukes have shrunk to walnuts under the jewelled
crust of their robes:
That millionaire is a mottled skin stuffed with bank-
notes.
And I saw a raging Don Quixote ride out again
And a hundred grey-bearded horsemen of the Apoca-
lypse
Scything the young men and the young trees behind
them.
And then I saw the dope-fiend aeronaut dropping
fully-fleshed out of the purple skirt and dusty lace of an
old monsignore. A moment later *his* belly-button gaped
to volley forth whole marching battallions of young
men in black, glassy gaiters. Sturm-Abteilungen!
Schutz-Staffel! Their military boots slap the tarry
summer road of the capital and their barking songs
shake the birds out of the lime-trees.
Good-bye to you, as well, my vast indifferent Mutter
As I turn away to the north to receive
Cries of scorn at school,
Sweaty gym shoes on my chin,
A hare-lip shuddering and sputtering,
Cold-sausage fingers at my flies.
  A mess of the bright brains of a little puss!
  Not I! Never! No, I never did!
  So why must I step from the hearth again and reach
  up, by your pitiless orders, into this trellis of rough,
  sooty bones?
  And now I hear again—I knew! I knew it!—
  The roaring fires break below,
  And I bounce again on the green tongues of flame
  And yell again on the punishing tips of fire.
  And I'm a midget burning in the gas-fire
  But seeing, out there, though my eyes sizzle,

Both of you squatting on the hearth,
Both of you squatting,
Gazing your greedy swill at me as I burn,
As I burn up,
As my burn blisters,
As my . . .
You, soldier of the late wars,
Reddened by war—A RED!—
Balefully grin from the hearth,
Delighting, absolutely, in, absolutely,
The burning of poor Abbervile.
And *you*, lady of the snakes, hissing,
Because my heel bruised you as I, frankly, *bolted*.
Seven coils of Janet on the hearth, and then
The hooded head raised on the last waving three feet of
her.
    And yet, yet, my dear gorgon, leave me *not*;
    Oh do *not*, my dear demon,
    Ghost away now from the hearth and doorward dim
    To leave me unobserved in these flames.
    Oh to leave me so,
    Oh alone, unwitnessed, seen by none as I burn to bits.
Flames roar between us, Carews, Carews!
Gas blue and sulphur-yellow, Mr and Mrs Carew!
Fever-pink, orange and green.
And now, at his last gasp, nobody sees him nor
On any enflamed eyeball does his tiny image flicker,
Upside-down.
Oh, oh, he's going out! He is . . .
    You? Who? You!
Through hell's annihilation peering;
Through the poison flames reaching, till
I'm pulled up by the cool, strong hand
Of the Maid from Manchester, until my eyeballs cool
On an ant scaling a gold hair
On the brown calf of a sun-bemused girl,
And bees lurching in the cowslips.

And I smell a sweet, childish soap,
Crushed thyme,
The breathing waters of Isis.
And I hear the summer water thudding down
Into the weedy hollow of a lock.
   Then listen, my riparian love,
   Oh bird who sang and raised the sun
   On married love and gardening days,
   (Saying goodbye without regret or animosity
   To this implacable grey city)
   Listen to the songs I sing in honour of that virtue:
   In honour of Hope I shall sing to you until the evening.

I. Lead your Orpheus from his hell,
  Eurydice, child of the bright earth.
  Lead him back, Eurydice,
  To a stone place on a summer day.
    But after that homecoming
    Dream away from brick and stone.
    Ride, in a dream of Orpheus,
    On the white horses of Chirico.
  We listened to that historical saint,
  Sir and comrade in St Giles.
  We heard the words of the burnt saint
  Hushing the whole market-place.
    Climbing the stair to an open door;
    Saying good-bye in a southern room.
    Fly from this window, Eurydice,
    Southward, over spawning rivers.

See how the spires are falling: Bernard hobbles down the High:
A rented house falls on the hill, and an old dog's adying.

II. Oh earthly Maid of Manchester
  Who changed the legend of Eurydice,

Who saved me from eternal fire,
Who brought me—you sublunary one!—
Back from a fantasy of fire
To these arches and to this hour.
   And yet this dear substantial maid
   Shall dream as well; she shall be drawn
   Into this dream of the salt shore.
   Dreaming her way through brick and chimney,
   Riding beside me over the shore
   On a white horse powdered with salt.
But in the softly-humming glow
At twilight she has listened to
The hermit's inflammatory words.
Gnats hummed in the elm-trees
And marvellous cars behind our backs
Hummed towards the capital.
   Climbing the familiar stair,
   Standing at the door, hand in hand,
   Awaiting, awaiting the judgement of Matthew.
   But after tea and Matthew's cloudy
   Haruspication of the teacups,
   Take our flight across the meadows.

A dying dog, damn it: he shakes to death in a cold corner:
A rented house, and unbequeathed: hear the window shudder.

III. You who reversed the joyless tale of Eurydice,
   Who led me from the nowhere of my hell
   To time for tea and the stone shade of arches—
   Fleshly girl, creature of time and place,
   Come to me here, where the laughter of young men
   Trumpets from the spiral stair behind me,
   And where I tramp in the cool shade of arches.
   There! *There* she runs, my heavy beauty!
     But fly from the woken earth before we climb
     To Matthew's room to talk of separations.

Ride this salt shore to the fruit of the sun
Which flames across the wings of oyster-catchers.
Snuffle the shore with flared and equine nostrils;
Receive the mist of tar, guano and salt.
Up, up, lovely equestrienne!
My circus beauty, jump this breakwater!
Remember too, maid of sweet memories,
The night when Peter the Hermit's fist was raised
Against the yellow stone of John the Baptist.
How he cried in the wilderness of crumbled colleges
Over the hum of the gnats and cars that hummed
And peered with headlights down the blue road.
His face peeled by the fires of an old war
This orator proclaims a holy war.

His hair ruffled by the raking fingers of thought,
Holding her teacup to the southern window
Delphic Matthew murmurs his ambiguities.
A breeze of roses—roses and anchovies.
(Oh tangled remembrancers of shore and sunrise!)
But we shall fly, the merlin and the pippit,
Over the downland's white archaic horses
And white seas, southward, raging at the foreland.

The old towers are falling down, and an old dog is dying:
A rented house and unbequeathed: how the window shudders!

iv. She brought him back from those eternal blue
Flames of the nursery gasfire, and she showed him
Time and the sun moving across the tower
And time's servants laughing from the stairs.
The fists of willows sprout along the river;
Antlers sprout on the foreheads of the fallow-deer;
A puff-of-cannon cloud is blown between
The crumbling pinnacles of the bell-tower.

And now, as teatime falls from the air, the hot
Ungainly beauty runs to the sound of bells.
  But though your capable bosom swells against me
  And falls again (with a sweet breath of mangers),
  Yet I shall pull this girl of flesh and time
  Into my endless dream of the salt shore.
  Your face rimed with the salt of sweat and sea
  You jump your sea-horse over the rotted spars
  Upended here in broken shells and conches,
  Whorls of pink; oyster- and scallop-shell—
  The mineral rubbish of a dying sea.
  Oh from this wilderness of salt and shell
  Up, up Bellerophon, to the red fruit of the sun!
But when you wake again at dead of day
To all the sly mortalities of the land,
A world gone bad with age and injustice,
Listen again to the scarred don preaching
His mutinous and holy sermons; how
He told us of that deathly, one-eyed general
Who shrieked in the ecclesiastical city
"Viva la Muerte!" and the deadly cry
Was echoed by a thousand seminarists,
A thousand cornets of the skull's hussars.
  Love-grappled birds on two wings soaring,
  The hawk and pippet take their nuptial flight
  From the elegant room and the prophetic friend.
  And by this loving denial of their natures,
  My winged Eurydice, my taloned songster,
  The coupled birds shall beat their locked wings
  Louder than all the guns of Spain, or hollow
  Drone from yellow, academic skulls.
  Their song has drowned the husky comminations
  Even of that dying and loveless professor.

The old towers are falling down, and an old dog's adying:
A rented house, and unbequeathed; an old dog dying.

v. It was King Lucifer
    Who whistled me back again
    To that sulphurous
    Nursery punishment.
        (But the maid long ago
        Put out the gas-fire.)
    It was King Mortimer,
    Gardener of salt fruit,
    Who called us into his dream
    Kingdom of the seashells.
        (But everybody knows
        That no dream is shared.)
    It was the King Fisher
    Who fished for us raucously,
    Crying that love required
    Our service in that war.
        (But I saw him smile in the lamplight
        As he mixed death with love.)
    Now all the kings are gone.
    Come away, come away,
    Breathing burden of love,
    Panting bird of the sun.
        (Leave, for the wars of love,
        This alexandrian city.)

Old   *Yes, well, he leaves much to be explored further*
Abberville   *Another day;*
                More questions than these
    To be answered,
    To be crassly avoided,
    Or simply to be superseded.
        As for the old prof, you need to hear no more of him
        Except that he did indeed slump
        Into ten concluding years of fruitless rage,
        Barren, repetetive self-pity.
        Dick, I take it, received whatever he needed

From all that preposterous gilding
Of past ages and dead faces,
And all that noisy abuse of the new age.
We'll leave the young man, now, with his dear maid,
The grocer's daughter,
Half-persuaded that he loves no less
Every poor devil in all the world who fights
The great gold tortoises of age and wealth.
And now I'm six days gone towards my dissolution:—
My release?
Do you conceive it possible, dear Olaf,
That as I reach the end of my long confabulation
I shall be somehow, magically, awarded
The honied serenity of a dying sage, and shed
All this cold frenzy of terrible boredom whenever I dwell upon
Whenever, even now, I anticipate
My own tongue-tied, everlasting absence?
Pale hands gently uplifted, eh?
A murmured benison for you?
Ha!